SAIL TO
FREEDOM

We dedicate this book to our children, Shirley and
Christopher, who let us leave home without complaint
and who have looked after our mail and diverse other
matters during our sojourn aboard and abroad.

SAIL TO FREEDOM

A practical guide to extended cruising

BILL *and* JUNE RAPER

FERNHURST BOOKS

First published 1993
by Fernhurst Books, 33 Grand Parade, Brighton, East Sussex BN2 2QA

Printed and bound in Great Britain

British Library Cataloguing in Publication Data
A catalogue record for this book is available from the British Library.

ISBN 0-906754-91-7

Photographic credits
All photographs were taken by the authors, and printed by Julia Claxton.

Edited by John Woodward
Designed by Jenny Searle
DTP by Jenny Searle
Cover design by Simon Balley
Printed by Ebenezer Baylis & Son, Worcester.

CONTENTS

PREFACE

We jointly count some 85 years of cruising: Bill since 1946 and June since marriage in 1956 (she little knew what she was letting herself in for!) For almost the whole of this period we have owned a cruising yacht of some sort — occasionally and injudiciously two at once — so we have plenty of experience. Yet despite this, and despite the fact that we planned most carefully for our sail-away years, we still managed to get some things wrong. So it is our aim in this book to pass on many of the lessons we have learned the hard way, including both the ordinary "makee-learn" accumulated during our years of cruising and our more recently adopted roving lifestyle.

Don't, we beg you, be put off by the apparent problems, by the costs, or by our lists — least of all by our lists. Trim your expenses as you would trim your sails to suit the state of the day and always with seamanlike prudence. Finally, if alas you are still in the dreaming stage, then don't give up: even dreams have a magical way of becoming reality if you stay with them.

We wish you all sunny skies and calm seas, halcyon days and balmy nights and, above all, the quiet satisfaction of doing what you really want to do. That's worth far more than the inevitable but transient problems. We know, for we have savoured it all to the full.

June and Bill Raper
Ros Arcan
Nice, France

1 DREAMS AND DECISIONS

Is this what you want to do?

- Motivation
- Expectations
- Actuality
- Mental attitudes

This is an important chapter: you must not skip or ignore it if you wish to give your project every chance of being happy and successful. There are a number of ports around the world where cherished dreams have finally been abandoned because they were not thought out properly in the initial stages: they can be recognised by the sorry, neglected boats forlornly awaiting buyers.

Motivation

It helps to think deeply about motivation, for this plays a part in determining your objectives which are fundamental to many of the important planning decisions. Your motivation may be dissatisfaction with your present lot; to realize a deep-rooted ambition; to see and do 'something' before settling down to a career (or a rocking chair); to overcome a personal setback such as an illness, bereavement, divorce or redundancy and so on. Whatever your motives, analyze them carefully and consider whether they are valid, and how they affect your objectives.

Expectations

So what are you are hoping to find? Relief from the madding crowd? Are you dreaming of seeing new lands and new peoples, perhaps with an interestingly different outlook and way of life? Do you look forward to making new, like-minded friends of many and diverse nationalities? Is your vision one of boundless good sailing and a release from stress; of peaceful days and starlit scented nights in quietly beautiful anchorages? Do you enjoy quiet satisfaction from achievement — however modest? Do you sometimes dreamingly feel the lure of the horizon?

Actuality

Most of us are dreamers at some time and you may have found yourself nodding in agreement with our notions. You may also have made allowance for excessive romanticism! If so, you will have been sensible. Nevertheless, we believe that if you have properly assessed your reasons for wanting to sail away for a time, you certainly will find most if not all of your expectations becoming a reality.

Some parts of the Mediterranean and Caribbean are, alas, scarcely serene any longer. Many of their peoples have been profoundly affected by the mass-tourist

LEFT *The authors' present yacht* Ros Arcan.

industries and, while we must applaud the better lifestyles that the tourists' money finances, we can only regret the greed, dishonesty and unhappiness which it seems to induce in many of the more popular tourist resorts. Yet just around the headland you may find a quiet, unspoilt spot and the naturally charming people you hoped to meet.

Our happiest tales and fondest memories are of such people: for instance the villagers who were so anxious to give a present to the first foreign yacht to visit their little port that, after pressing us to declare what we needed, induced us to opt for a loaf of bread as being simple and undemanding. They then proceeded to go around every house collecting a little bread here and a little there because their bakery had sold out by the time we arrived. Or the ten-year old fisher boy who insisted we accept a polished crab-claw which was to him a prized good luck charm.

The weather will not always give idyllic sailing — even the trade winds can become over-enthusiastic — but more likely you will find yourselves doing far more motor-sailing than you anticipated. It pays to have a powerful engine and not to be shy of using it. Whether you arrive under sail or power, you will certainly see places which otherwise you would not have visited; you may not even have known they existed.

You will also meet many people of all nationalities doing just what you are doing, so you will not be alone or even remotely unique. Some, perhaps like you, will be just pottering; others will be circumnavigating, maybe even on their second or third time round! There's no elitism among the real yachties — both coast-potterer and ocean sailor are part of the cruising fraternity, equally willing to turn-to and help rather than merely advise from behind their beer. As for the locals — if you are polite and considerate, and if you can resist telling them what they should be doing with their lives, then you will always be welcome.

Mental attitudes

You must conduct a rigorous, searching and totally honest examination of your own attitudes. We must stress that it would be very imprudent and short-sighted of you not to do this. Also, there must be complete frankness, honesty and openness between all partners. Have you never been pleased to get home from a cruise? (We don't mean from a nasty passage). Do you *really* want to go away from everything you know at home and not see it again for

months or even a year or two? How will you cope with living week-in week-out with your partner(s) in the confines of a small boat? Are you prepared to compromise with good grace? Will you suffer from personal claustrophobia? What about your partner(s)? Are they as fully committed as you or just supporting you out of love or loyalty?

You will not really be able to test all of these aspects before you sail: not even a couple of months on a foreign charter cruise will search them out. Talk them through freely and frankly — if the proposed cruise is not going to work it's better to know before you slip your moorings and set sail.

2 BACKGROUND PLANNING
Practical considerations

- Who does it?
- What about the children?
- The hearth and home
- Residency
- Money
- Health
- Insurance
- Communications
- Crisis and catastrophe

Who does it?

Everyone does it: young couples, families having a mid-career break, victims of redundancy awaiting better times, and retired older people. There is no upper age limit: we know people coming up to their eighties who are still cruising full-time and have no thoughts of moving ashore. Even people whose health isn't all that good enjoy the lifestyle, although generally they are careful not to get too far away from reliable medical aid. You'll find burghers and burglars, publicans and plumbers, the have's and the barely have's. The sea is a great leveller — it soaks the prince and the pauper alike — and this is one of the reasons why the floating communities are so helpful and friendly.

But are you ready yourself? Have you a number of years of successful cruising behind you or are you fairly new to sailing?

Have you a qualification of some value, such as an RYA/DTI Yachtmaster or U.S. Coastguard Certificate: a qualification obtained via meaningful examination and not just a bureaucratic form in return for a fee? Should you attend a practical course afloat? Or maybe spruce up your navigation by attending a winter evening's course? Or would it be a good idea to join an experienced crew for a couple of long passages or offshore races to gain more practical experience? How about attending one of the diesel engine maintenance courses often set up by engine manufacturers? Have you a VHF Operator's certificate? Should you obtain a certificate allowing you to operate on the MF/HF radiotelephone bands, or an amateur radio operator's certificate?

It may all sound a bit formidable but it must make sense, it tests your commitment and, importantly, it is fun.

What about the children?

It goes without saying that the needs of children are a very serious consideration indeed. Children are astonishingly adaptable and resilient but you mustn't let this seduce you into thinking that the life is ideal for them and that they'll inevitably grow up into great young people. You have to consider their education and — particularly with teenagers — their social needs.

Onboard education up to the age of about twelve seems to be commonplace and practical; provided the parents are responsible and recognise their obligations, the educational levels attained appear to be good.

For the over-twelves you have to think a bit harder: there are examinations to consider and you are unlikely to be able to educate your own child to examination standard in all the necessary subjects. Make enquiries and seek advice in your home country: you will probably find that there are several institutions which provide school education to examination levels by correspondence lessons. These programmes are usually sufficiently flexible in scheduling to accommodate the rather erratic cruising communications. They do, however, demand strict parental cooperation, both in maintaining regular hours of study and in encouraging and assisting the child — often using guidance notes supplied.

It is usual for full-time "cruisers" to spend periods of several months in one place during the winter, the hurricane season and so on. During such times it is often possible for the children to attend a local school — very often an "expatriate" one or a school in which tuition is primarily given in the English language.

Education apart, long-term cruising can cause social problems for teenagers. The few we have met on our travels have tended to miss the companionship of their peers. We personally feel that any child should experience some "normal" life ashore and the thought of children spending (say) ten years afloat is rather disturbing. Children living ashore spend a large part of their lives under the control of teachers and coexisting with other kids. Children living on a cruising yacht will occasionally get away with other children, but despite this they are likely to become insufferably precocious from a surfeit of adult company. Their 'childhood' is at risk, and while they will benefit from all sorts of experiences not available to their shore-based peers, they also stand to lose facets of childhood that ultimately shape the adult.

The hearth and home

It is very difficult to advise on what to do about your present home as it is such a uniquely personal matter. Weigh up the prospects of being able to buy back into the housing market when the time comes to move back ashore and bear in mind the very high cost of storing furniture and effects. Or do you need to sell to release capital for the venture? Even if selling

BELOW *Could you cope with a mechanical breakdown at sea?*

seems a good option, it probably makes a lot of sense to hang on to your house for a year or two after you set sail in case the life palls more quickly than you thought it would, or some unexpected crisis (for example, over-optimistic budgeting) requires you to return home.

Think about a long lease-out of your house — it may have beneficial tax effects and produce income (though this will probably be taxed in the country of origin). If you are planning in terms of returning home at fairly regular intervals, you could perhaps keep your present home in "mothballs", rent it out short-term (but this has some horrific potential dangers) or move to a smaller property to release capital while retaining a foothold in the property market.

Residency

Your departure for extensive cruising will not affect your right to resume residence unless you only had restricted rights in the first place. There may well be advantage in negotiating with the tax authorities a revised status; in the UK, for example, that of "not resident and not normally resident". This will exempt you from paying tax on income not earned in the country such as from investments abroad. Each country has its own rules and the USA, for example, is much more restrictive. There may be restrictions placed on the length of time you can spend in the country concerned in any one tax year and you may forfeit some other benefits. The whole tax question is a minefield and you should take advice from several quarters. Bear in mind that you will be an "oddity" to many professional people and their initial reaction may well be discouraging: persevere and press your points until you are satisfied your case has been thoroughly researched.

Money

We are assuming that you propose to maintain a bank account, but is it best held in your home country or elsewhere? Assuming you retain your citizenship a home bank account is probably the best option, but the means by which you are going to draw money when abroad is worthy of some thought and investigation. As we see it, the following are the alternatives open to you.

Traveller's Cheques These are secure and convenient but they are an expensive option. They tie up your cash without any compensating interest, there is a commission to pay both on buying and on cashing them, and who can lay out enough cash to meet their requirements for six months at a time or probably longer? You might hold a smallish amount in this form as an emergency fund, but remember that they have a finite period of validity.

Letters of Credit These are cheaper and less expensive than Travellers's Cheques but they demand a high credit rating with your bank, are not likely to be used conveniently in out-of-the way places and are generally cumbersome.

Inter-bank transfers If you are to be stationary in one place for some time, inter-bank transfers can certainly be considered. In many places it is possible to open a local bank account which can be held in a foreign currency, and any balance can be transferred elsewhere without difficulty.

There are, of course, charges to be paid for the transfer but in our experience the main disadvantage is the deliberate slowness of the banking systems. At one point we arranged a bank transfer instruction to pay our monthly marina berthing charges during the winter lay-by. When

we came to sail on, we found that our account was seven weeks in arrears and naturally the marina was not prepared to let us go. The UK bank declared the transfer had been made and it could not help further; the local branch of the Spanish bank "knew nothing of it" and claimed that their Madrid head office did not hold the credit either. The problem was eventually resolved with the help of our club's local representative but it is totally clear that deliberate delay had been built into the system giving one or other (or probably both) Banks free use of the cash for a considerable period. So beware.

Eurocheques Although primarily limited to Europe, the Eurocheque system is very effective and is not particularly expensive. It does, of course, require that you hold an account with a participating bank who will issue identity cards and Eurocheques against payment of an annual fee. When you cash a cheque abroad you make it out in the local currency and there should be no charge or commission levied by the bank where you cash the cheque. Your "home" bank will make a relatively small charge for negotiating the cheque when it is eventually presented to them and makes its turn on the currency exchange.

This exchange process is a minor irritation since, although you know the relative values of the two currencies at the time you draw the foreign coin, you do not know the rate that will be applied in due course. Nevertheless, Eurocheques are a convenient, viable and generally easy way to draw cash. You can also use them to pay bills and make purchases, although beware of some suppliers demanding a premium "as our bank charges us..."

Postcheques The cash system operated by many postal authorities (e.g. Postbank/Girobank) is very convenient and is available in virtually all European countries; Iceland; Greenland and the Faroes; Malta; Turkey; Cyprus; Egypt and some other North African countries (but subject to some restrictions); Israel; Madeira and the Azores; the Canaries; the French Colonies of Guiana, Martinique, Reunion, St. Pierre and Miquelon; Thailand; Hong Kong and Japan.

You must have a suitable Post Office/Girobank account (in credit!) after which you can obtain a Postcheque Card and Postcheques for overseas use. Producing the card and writing a cheque in your own language using the local

currency will enable you to obtain cash at almost any Post Office. Needless to say there are maximum limits and we have found that some post offices in very rural areas will only pay out the maximum! Nevertheless, the system is an excellent standby although the cheques cannot be used in retail or similar outlets.

Credit card advances We have found credit card advances — principally using Visa — to be the most reliable and cost-effective method of obtaining running finance, provided that you avoid incurring the penal interest charged on overdue accounts. Most companies will accept instructions to debit your "base bank account" with the monthly amounts due so helping you to avoid paying interest or mis-estimating the remittance required if the account does not reach you in time for specific action. Although Visa Card rules vary somewhat, a handling charge of 1.5% seems to be normal. You must also take into account the exchange rate uncertainty which applies to all forms of foreign cash transactions, but this disadvantage is offset by the convenience of the system.

Emergency cache

We would advise that you have a modest emergency cache of an acceptable currency tucked away under the bunk or somewhere. In Europe, this should be in U.S. dollars, pounds sterling or German marks; elsewhere dollars or sterling might be better, with dollars having the slight edge despite their recent volatility. You never know when an acceptable cash payment may be needed in return for an emergency service.

Supplementing your income

Unless you have particular skills in universal demand, don't rely on making much income on the way. Many countries prevent freelance working by non-nationals; if you are an engineer, a good carpenter, electrician, electronics technician or are just generally skilful on boats you will be able to pick up some "unofficial" work but look upon any such income as a bonus and be discreet. Sometimes opportunities arise on the yacht delivery market if you can make your availability known, and if you have skills which are saleable on a temporary basis, for example in the computer industry, you can perhaps return home during the off-season to restore the bank balance.

Writing, while it can be satisfying personally, will not earn very much; the market is generally over-subscribed and it should be considered as a bonus if you sell.

Do not rely on chartering as a source of additional income unless you intend to do it on a virtually full-time basis. It is extremely hard work and it will affect your costs quite considerably by increasing your insurance premium, requiring the services of an agent to advertise your yacht, possibly involving payment of local taxes and so on. It calls for a fairly full season of bookings to make it worthwhile. Moreover, some countries have devised a variety of imaginative bureaucratic obstacles which can make life difficult and the occasional charter simply not worthwhile. In Turkey — and elsewhere — even allowing genuine guests to contribute to expenses via a 'kitty' has been held to constitute a charter so keep very quiet if you follow this common practice.

Health

It makes sense to have a medical check before you set off, making sure that the doctor knows about the life you intend to lead. Have any necessary vaccinations/inoculations that he may recommend — some areas still have problems with endemic diseases such as cholera or malaria.

Seriously consider health-care insurance but thoroughly investigate the market with the various companies immediately involved as well as with one or two really good insurance brokers. It is astonishing how widely premiums and benefits can vary — by up to 100% for the identical cover is not exceptional.

Check out the extent of reciprocity between various countries' national health schemes — you will probably find that things are not always as straightforward as you might expect. For example, if you are accepted by your taxation people as being "non-resident" it may debar you from free or subsidised health treatment in other countries unless you are formally resident there. This is certainly the case within the "Common" Market. Repatriation insurance is available and if you are proposing to visit backward countries it might be well worth investigating cover to fly you to suitable facilities should proper treatment not be available locally. Review the financial adequacy of your cover at least every two years or so as medical costs are very susceptible to above-average inflation. For a suitable onboard medical kit see Chapter 7.

Insurance

In addition to considering health insurance, look closely at covering your other assets (and not only against sunburn!) After all, you have a great deal of your capital tied up in the boat. Generally underwriters won't consider "total loss only" cover, but world-wide third party cover is obtainable very reasonably.

Shop around for the best all-round deal: premiums payable and available geographic cover can vary widely and surprisingly. But in attempting to identify the best deal, do not be over-influenced by the "special concessions" given by some underwriters/brokers to members of specific yacht clubs or associations; the premiums payable and cover received can invariably be bettered elsewhere. You must obviously look at the premium levels and geographic cover, but you must also compare the cover given under the hull clauses. Try to ascertain the standard of claims service given by the broker: you may be able to check this on the "grapevine" or obtain first-hand experience from a yacht surveyor. Remember that your broker needs to have good international representation.

In Europe, bear in mind that Italy not only demands valid third party cover but requires this to be documented in a special manner, in Italian, and it must specifically confirm the cover is valid in Italy. If you do not conform, you are likely to be held pending confirmation that you are insured or that you have obtained acceptable cover in Italy (at a steep local premium).   Elsewhere, it is not unusual to be asked by some marinas for evidence of third party cover but this rarely leads to complications.

If you are going to sail short or single-handed, particularly on long or frequent overnight passages, ensure your underwriter is aware of the fact and accepts it. Bear in mind the pitfalls of under-insuring. If you 'write down' your valuations to save premium and are later unfortunate enough to make a claim, your insurers are fully entitled to carry out their own valuation and settle pro-rata according to the extent of your under-declaration.

Bear in mind potential customs liabilities: a yacht becoming a total loss inside some territorial waters is considered to have been "imported" by the customs administration and duty levied accordingly. Ensure your policy covers this eventuality — and also that the costs of wreck removal are covered. Despite what we have written earlier, some policies linked to club membership are very advantageous in these respects — the Seven Seas Cruising Association scheme is a case in point. There are also some brokers who can arrange foreign cruising cover at attractive rates and with realistic conditions. In Europe, at present, the German "Pantaenius" organisation (which also has a UK subsidiary) is particularly notable.

Don't forget suitable cover — within the yacht policy or separately — for your personal effects, cameras etc. Credit/cash cards are probably best insured with one of the special companies in the field, as not only are you then indemnified against the consequences of their loss or theft, but it only takes one telephone call to cancel the cards and arrange for new ones (and interim emergency cash if necessary).

Communications

Reliable reception of mail can be difficult to arrange and mail transit time hard to gauge (except that it will take longer than you expect!). Marinas will generally hold mail for you but tell them you are on the way. Some port authorities will also do so but frequently in haphazard way. Local representatives of some clubs/associations will hold mail but it is polite if possible to ask them beforehand.

The postal authorities' Poste Restante services are variable: in some places they are highly unreliable, insecure or (in France) expensive. Always ask on two or more days and try to think how your mail may be pigeon-holed — by surname, by boat name, by Christian name if used in the address, or even by initials! If you have access to mail pigeon holes, make sure you look in each one: letters are often mistakenly placed.

As for forwarding from home, the family will probably do it but bear in mind that they will be away for periods and it will be a demanding chore for them. Many people use professional mail forwarding services — they will often also arrange payment of accounts, forwarding of spares etc. provided they are kept in funds.

Fax is now very widely available and generally reliable. In our experience, fax is cheaper and safer than the telephone for business affairs, faster by far than mail and very convenient all round. We often find newsagents, travel agents and photocopy shops will send and receive a fax with less fuss and more cheaply than post offices. Many hotels provide telephone, telex and fax facilities but we have found that they tend to be expensive.

Telephone services are also improving, with card phones available in many countries. British Telecom, A.T.& T. and other administrations also operate "home-base" billing systems which are well worth following through. With these systems you are given a personal account number and an identification code, enabling you to contact your home country operator with a minimum coin insertion and deal direct thereafter.

If you have VHF or HF radio you can use link call services via convenient Coast Radio Stations, but this usually works out quite expensive (also see Chapter 6). Again, some telephone administrations have special domestic schemes which do work out somewhat cheaper than the usual international processes but, in our view, the shoreside telephone box or public phone centre are still the simplest and cheapest options.

We do recommend that you take some time to plan your communications carefully, as being out of touch is the cause of much unnecessary unhappiness and worry.

Crisis and catastrophe

Of course, we all hope neither will strike, but don't pretend there isn't a risk. It could be medical — see above re insurance. It could be loss of your boat through sea peril — again see our insurance comments above but think about how you'll get home. It may be months before the underwriters pay up. Serious damage to the boat can also take a long time to fix and for your claim to be settled. We know of one yacht whose rudder skeg was damaged and although the underwriters acknowledged their liability for repairs the owners were still living on board on the hard six months later trying to get some physical action.

Try to have access to some emergency funds, just in case. This may be too much for the "in-house" resources in which case a "with-profits" endowment life policy could be a good and cash-efficient starter if it has loan value. The interest rate payable is probably as cheap as any you are likely to be able to find and the option of if and when to repay the capital borrowed is yours provided you keep up the interest payments or ensure there is residual loan value against which interest can be charged. For this reason alone it seems to make sense to retain any "with profits" life assurance policies you might have, but it's worth taking financial advice (see Chapter 8 re copying important documents).

3

THE RIGHT YACHT
Choosing a boat for the job

- **Type**
- **Rig**
- **Engine**
- **Deck layout**
- **Accommodation**
- **Outline specification**

Type

Clearly, the first and easiest decision is whether your choice is a sailing or motor yacht. Most of the comments hereafter apply to both, and here we are using "type" to refer to style rather than the principal form of propulsion.

Firstly let's look at size, which governs the quality of life on board. About 30 ft (9 m) seems to be the most practical minimum overall length of hull for lengthy co-habitation. A recent survey of some 50 cruising yachts wintering in Larnaca, Cyprus (to which we shall make several useful references in this book) found an average overall length of 40 ft with 11.8 ft beam (12.3 x 3.6 m).

Try to resist the temptation to stretch to that rather larger beauty that you covet and to fiddle your budget to justify her: the odds are that your budget will be exceeded anyway in practice and some prudent leeway is strongly advised. On the other hand, if you can afford a larger yacht than the two of you have previously handled, don't be put off by the increased size. In many ways, a larger boat is easier to handle than a smaller one: there is probably an easier motion for working on deck, she will not blow off on the wind quite so quickly when manoeuvring, she will carry her way better; in short, there seems to be more time to do everything (though you do land harder if you get it wrong!).

As to construction material, GRP is clearly the most common nowadays, but wood and steel are also common and popular. Ferro-cement and aluminium are encountered but problems — even minor damage — may present repair difficulties however well built and maintained the ship might be. Your ship will be hard-used: in many ways, wood has distinct advantages when it comes to the inevitable

repairs. You may worry about the depredations of teredo worm or gribble, but provided you keep the hull well anti-fouled there is really little to worry about in our view. We don't rank worm in the same league as the dreaded pox — osmosis — or an unprovoked attack of electrolysis. We do strongly recommend that you have a planned maintenance schedule and keep a log of what you do and when you do it (see Chapter 8).

The hull design is a matter of individual preference, although ruggedness, stability and an easy motion are obviously more important than potential speed and the ability to turn on a sixpence. Exhilarating performance may be fun for a fortnight but it can prove wearing in the long term.

Will your current boat suit? Review her in the light of what follows in this chapter and later.

Rig

What you are used to should and no doubt will play a strong part in your choice but the following brief comments may give food for thought.

Sloop/cutter Such rigs are simple and efficient but each sail is relatively large — can they be handled by one person? Furling headsails are commonplace now and there is no doubt that they make life very much easier. However, we retain strong reservations about furling mainsails be they "in-mast" or "in-boom": they still fall into the hi-tech category in our catalogue and if anything goes wrong with them at sea, it demands a large strong crew or drastic destructive action to sort it out. In general, you should avoid hi-tech rigs since they can be difficult and expensive to maintain, and may require the services of a specialist.

Ketch/yawl These rigs are very popular and both give useful combinations of sail which are easy to handle. The ketch rig is arguably better as its mizzen is more efficient than that of the yawl as well as being more likely to be

wholly inboard, making it easier and safer to handle. Be she a yawl or a ketch, a mizzen staysail is a worthy sail to have aboard: genoa, mizzen staysail and mizzen is a worry-free combination when you have a chance to set it.

Schooner This rig seems to be growing in popularity. The staysail schooner is an efficient rig and the sails are individually easy to handle.

The Larnaca survey found the popularity ratings to be sloop followed by ketch, with cutter a poor third. Whichever rig you choose, you will find that very few full-time cruising people bother with a spinnaker. Frankly, setting it up when short-handed is an avoidable hassle, its gear clutters the deck (you will find deck space is at a premium anyway) and, finally, a boomless cruising 'chute is far more practical if you are not racing.

Engine

You will need a thoroughly reliable diesel auxiliary of sufficient power to punch into head seas, for you will motor or motor-sail a great deal more than you will expect at this stage. Petrol engines are now rarities and we wouldn't have one aboard as a propulsion unit. The conventional shaft and stern tube layout seems preferable to the "Z" or "saildrive" systems, being easier to maintain and repair while afloat.

ABOVE Albatros, *built in 1907 as a steam-powered torpedo tender and now converted into a live-aboard yacht.*

As with rigs, avoid the exotic.

A motor yacht should be twin-engined or have a wing engine for emergency use; alternatively have a workable sail rig to make port if your engine is immobilised. If finances run to it, one of the cutting blade systems is worth fitting to the propeller shaft as you will frequently encounter floating lines and nets which can foul your stern gear.

Deck layout

You should give serious consideration to your comfort at sea. Do you enjoy regular dollops of water being thrown at you every time you turn to windward in a fresh breeze? (It's not obligatory except in the movies!) Do you have or could you fit an alternative steering position below? If you have a centre cockpit with a clear acrylic screen which you could convert into a weather-proof "wheelhouse" by rigging zip-fastened covers when necessary, do go ahead with the necessary fittings. Unfortunately, a rigid half-wheelhouse can be very hot when you are not at sea.

You will need to be able to rig sun awnings for general use while at anchor or alongside, and the helmsman and cockpit crew (at least) will benefit from having shelter

from the sun while under way. An awning for the coachroof should be easy to rig to give shade for living on deck. Awnings over the cockpit or "sitting-out" deck areas should have side screens which can be dropped down or be easily attached to shade you from the late afternoon sun.

Awnings should be made of fairly heavy and, if possible, ultra-violet proofed material. You need heavyweight cloth because the continual rustling of light stuff drives you crazy! The method of rigging the awnings should also be thought out carefully. You may need them even when the wind is a fresh Force 5, so they must be secure, but remember that speedy dismantling is a "must" — an awning full of wind could quickly take you out to sea if the breeze turns sharply into a blow (not unusually at three o'clock in the morning!).

Take a close look at your deck space — you will find it is a premium area in demand for sunbathing space, stowage of bicycles, gas bottles, sailboards, outboards, liferaft, passerelle (gangway — see later), dinghy and much else besides. You will find yourself entertaining on board so your cockpit (be it centre or aft) and sheltered deck space should be congenial for that purpose. Try to arrange space for up to (say) ten people for drinks and nibbles or for a crew of (say) four to eat in comfort. You may think you

TOP *An awning to give shade for living on deck is essential in a hot climate. This simple design is easy to rig but sturdy and effective.*

ABOVE *Deck space is always at a premium. Here a sailboard is neatly stowed by lashing it to the rail.*

TOP RIGHT A D.I.Y. *square wind scoop which catches the breeze from any direction.*

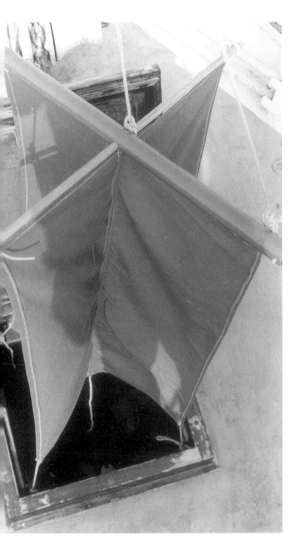

reversible electric fans fitted to them. If any of the cowl vents are sited where they can snag sheets — if they can they will — fit suitable guards.

Try to fit oscillating D.C. fans throughout the accommodation — the usual car type are cheap but perfectly adequate; indeed they are cheap enough for you to be able to carry a spare. Don't forget the poor cook — a fan in the galley contributes handsomely to a good meal.

You will have guests visit you on holiday and we believe that, unless it is quite impossible, it is very desirable that there is space for visitors to berth in a dedicated sleeping cabin well separated from the permanent crew, although an overflow into the saloon for sleeping is obviously acceptable on a short-term basis if unavoidable. The saloon itself should be capable of seating at least six people at the table in reasonable comfort

The "head" needs to be of reasonable size and should include a good shower which does not call for the removal of awkward floorboards or the covering of other fittings. W.C's now need to be capable of discharge into a holding tank; the use of holding tanks is not yet enforced in many places owing to the lack of shoreside discharge facilities but no doubt the requirement will spread. It is possible to get kits for D.I.Y. fitting of holding systems including a flexible tank and the necessary pipework and valves. Short-term alternatives are the self-contained types such as "Porta-potti" and the U.S. SeaLand systems; these are also very useful when you are living aboard on the hard (which you will do) and save having to trek through the night to the yard's W.C. If the principal sleeping cabin is aft, try hard to fit in a separate "head" there — at least a wash-hand basin and W.C.

It is essential to have plenty of locker stowage space. You would be surprised how much space actually is available if you look hard enough. It might only be suitable for rustless, sealed items such as plastic bottles of detergents or disinfectants, but moving those items will free space for other things. A bilge which only very occasionally gets wet can be used to stow lots of things if they are properly wrapped (clingfilm is useful for this).

Your ship will be your home so you'll want to make her as comfortable as possible below. You may want to turn a normally unused cabin into a hobby space or workshop. If the cockpit can be closed off with good awnings (perhaps incorporating plastic windows) to make

have more space than you can conceivably fill — but you'll be wrong!

Accommodation

This must be well ventilated. Check that you have sufficient good hatches and/or skylights which will allow any breeze to be directed into all parts of the ship. You will need to rig wind scoops: these can be purchased to stock designs or made to fit particular hatches. Ensure you have adequate cowl ventilators fitted onto water-trap boxes so that the ship is well ventilated even when at sea. Such ventilators over the galley and in the "heads" could well have

ABOVE *A windscreen-type half wheelhouse. The sides can be fitted with clear plastic to increase shelter.*

LEFT *A windscoop for below-deck ventilation.*

ABOVE RIGHT *An excellent awning with furling sides.*

a weatherproof area so much the better — it enables each partner to be alone for a while to do his or her "own thing" and this is important. You will recall that we have referred to the need (not the desirability) of being able to get away from each other for a while — here is one method!

Whew! We can almost hear you saying it: these guys expect all of this in a thirty-foot boat! Yes, we do and it is possible! Of course, it's easier to get it into a thirty-five footer...

Outline specification

Having run through the most important considerations you can now begin to build up the specification of the boat you would like to have. But still to be determined is the style of cruising you intend to enjoy. On the assumption that you will primarily be day-sailing along coastlines, we can perhaps use the following hypothetical parameters and develop a broad specification for a matching target yacht.

You will develop the process to flesh out your own needs as you read the later chapters. So, let us say you will:

- wish to live on board in reasonable comfort;
- potter along coast-wise in leisurely fashion;
- enjoy a really good sail (or passage) but avoid discomfort if possible;
- use the engine to punch into dead nosers or in very light winds;
- make overnight passages when necessary;
- make longer passages as necessary but probably rarely, if at all, over 500 miles;
- usually have only two people on board but with occasional guests and fairly frequent socialising with other crews.

From this, we can, as an example only, devise a very basic outline specification for a yacht of between 30 and 40 ft (9-12 m), medium-to-heavy displacement for easy motion, well-mannered and not tender, with four berths in two separate cabins, a rig of your preference, a diesel engine capable of driving her at 5-6 knots against a headwind of 15-20 knots with corresponding sea conditions and at a reasonable fuel consumption, and with a centre cockpit

which you can effectively make weatherproof using readily rigged dodgers and hood.

Having determined this broad outline, you can now decide whether your present boat is in the running or if you would be wise to look for another. You will have realised that many standard production yachts can be suitable — the classic Laurent Giles designs, Moodies, Westerlies, some of the Beneteau and Jeanneau models, Vancouvers, Rhodes and Alden cruisers and some of the better "Taiwan takeaways" for example.

You are unlikely to find exactly what you'd like so keep a smart weather eye open for a boat's potential. Very few live-aboard cruising yachts have not been modified by their owners, often to a substantial degree. Don't, however, rush into making major changes: you will probably find that your ideas will benefit from living on board and visiting other boats being used for the same purpose. Experience will also make you aware of other designs possibly better suited to your needs. In the Larnaca survey the average age of yacht was 15 years and the average length of ownership 8.5 years, so a new boat is not the fashion and most confirmed cruising folk have changed boats at least once.

4

FITTING HER OUT
Essentials

- Is she sound?
- The sails and standing rigging
- The engine and fuel
- Ground tackle
- Bilge pump
- Water
- Electricity
- Cooking and heating

Is she sound?

Whether you are keeping your present boat or are changing, you should consider having her surveyed. Of course, if you are buying a boat new to you, a survey will probably have been undertaken in any case. If you are keeping your current yacht, we think that a 'basic' survey of (at least) the hull and rigging is a good idea if only to satisfy yourself that all is well but more usefully, perhaps, if you find you want to change your insurers. Most underwriters will require a recent survey (certainly one not older than five years) before accepting a new risk.

If relevant, it's certainly worthwhile having the keel bolts X-rayed and, if she is a wooden boat, checking a few fastenings. Inspect the steering gear, including the rudder bearings. Examine her carefully for electrolysis and, if she is a GRP boat, for osmosis.

If you are worried about osmosis, it is handy to know that there are a few places around the globe where the boat can dry out slowly but surely over the winter months while you live aboard. D.I.Y. osmosis cure is a common practice at Larnaca Marina in Cyprus, for example. There are usually three or four boats on the hard for that purpose and the crews often form working parties to speed the application of the new gelcoat in the spring. The chandler on the Larnaca Marina hires out heavy-duty sanders, grinders and a moisture meter, and there always seems to be someone over-wintering who is genuinely knowledgable on the subject.

To return to the scene before you leave, go over the boat thoroughly yourself in addition to any survey. Surveyors do not necessarily spend much time checking non-structural fittings and this is something you can do better yourself. If she is your current boat, you know her well and if she is new to you, what better way to find out about her intimate details? Put to rights anything you suspect — it is so much easier to obtain the bits you need in your home port than to track them down in a strange place. In effect, carry out a very thorough fit-out — you will settle into your new lifestyle more comfortably if you don't have to attend to neglected or avoidable repairs in a foreign land within a short time of arriving.

The sails and standing rigging

Have the sails checked professionally and any defects made good. Should you replace any? This is not always cheap or easy in many good cruising grounds, although bear in mind that, as a transient boat, you are allowed to import "non-consumables" duty-free in many countries. This enables you to buy from, for example, Hong Kong at very favourable prices even after paying the air freight charges.

Have you a furling headsail? It will make an enormous difference to the sail-handling effort, which is especially important when you're sailing short-handed. If you have a cruising 'chute, you should consider a 'snuffer'. If your boat is a ketch or yawl, do investigate having a mizzen staysail. Consider fitting an easy reefing system if one is not already in use — either roller reefing (but avoiding complicated in-mast systems) or the resuscitated 'old-fashioned' slab reefing. Should you fit lazyjacks or a modern (and more expensive!) equivalent to make short-handed sail work easier?

Ensure that both the sail covers and the waster strip on furling sails are in good condition. The strong ultra-violet effect soon damages unprotected sails. Check your sail repair kit: it should contain needles, threads and twines, palm, suitable tape and pieces of appropriate sailcloth, spare luff and foot slides, etc.

Check over the standing rigging very carefully. Keep a couple of spare rigging screws on board plus sufficiently large wire shears, some lengths of flexible wire rope, a few suitable thimbles and "Bulldog" grips so you can make temporary rigging repairs if necessary. (We take it for granted that you regularly check the running gear and have appropriate spares such as rope, blocks, thimbles and shackles.)

The engine and fuel

Thoroughly check the engine(s). Have the injectors serviced or exchanged and get a spare set. Clean and check the fuel and cooling water systems and pumps. Get overhaul kits for the fuel lift pump(s) and water pumps. Perhaps carry spare fresh water circulating pump(s) and fuel lift pump(s). Carry out a full oil change and renew the fuel and lubricating oil filter elements before departure. Ensure you have several replacement fuel and water filter elements on board. Also stock up with other necessary spares such as gaskets and gasket material, thermostat(s), hoses, s/s hose clips (have plenty), drive and fan belts, greases and so on. (see Appendix 4).

Do you have the necessary service manuals and the names/addresses, telephone and fax numbers of the firm(s) which can send spares to you? Check you have all the necessary spanners, sockets and Allen keys in both imperial and metric sizes.

Fit engine/hour meter(s) if not already installed. We also consider it to be absolutely essential to fit an additional high-efficiency water/fuel filter to the engine fuel supply line (e.g. Dahl, Vetus, Fram). You will inevitably pick up dirty fuel somewhere along the way and the normal filters fitted to an engine just cannot cope with some of the contamination you will encounter. Don't forget to carry spare filter elements for it too.

Is the fuel tankage large enough? If at all possible, you should have enough capacity for about 1000 miles. Not only may this be necessary but it will also let you buy fuel at the cheapest ports — often duty-free (the cruising "network" will keep you advised on where these may be). Augment your tankage if necessary. You can now get flexible tanks suitable for fuel oil but you must be careful when installing them to ensure there is no risk of chafing or even puncturing if the tanks move as the boat works in a seaway. Rigid tanks are undoubtedly better if they can be arranged but we would recommend galvanised ones rather than stainless steel (the same goes for extra fresh water tanks).

Ground tackle

You will need two bowers as a minimum, one of which should — without any doubt at all — be a Fisherman pattern. The choice for the other(s) is really yours, between CQR, Danforth, Bruce or other patent designs. We have got along very well with a CQR which is self-stowing (psst — it sometimes needs a little help!) but whichever pattern attracts you, err on the generous side with its weight and the size of the chain. We assure you that in doubtful holding ground with a 'hoolie' blowing, you will bless having been generous. 'Old Coldnose' is as good as any insurance policy and pays off much more quickly!

Perhaps we should explain the need for a Fisherman: there are times when a patent anchor simply will not cut through a heavy weed bed or hook in to a bottom with only a shallow layer of sand or mud over rock. That's when you need the old tried and trusty, heavy and cumbersome Fisherman. Agreed, you may have a problem stowing it — a Fisherman has to be heavier than a patent anchor and arranging self-stowage is not easy but the handling problem is a small price to pay.

You will also need a kedge of reasonable size stowed and handled from aft for berthing bow-to or for holding the ship across the wind and into a swell.

Have enough anchor cable to lie in up to 20 metres of water (at high water) because some anchorages are very deep. Each of the two bowers in use should have its own cable, both because you should be able to lie to two anchors when necessary and because when you need to change from one anchor to the other it is faster and easier if you don't have to change the cable too.

It is your decision whether to use all chain or a combination of chain and rope on your bowers. The size and design of your boat may dictate this to some degree: she may simply be unable to stow enough suitable chain right up forward, more's the pity. However, there are lighter chains now available (at a price) which lie between conventional galvanised chain and anchor rope and will certainly last longer than the latter.

Bear in mind that the pull on an anchor should not be more than five degrees from the horizontal (five degrees

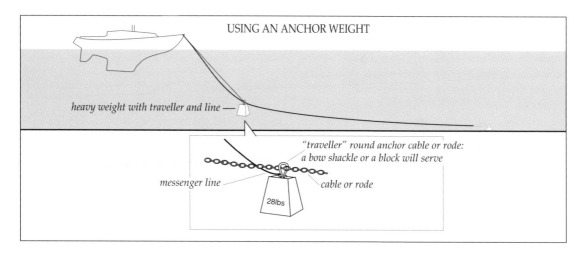

USING AN ANCHOR WEIGHT

heavy weight with traveller and line —

"traveller" round anchor cable or rode:
a bow shackle or a block will serve

messenger line

cable or rode

28lbs

reduces the holding power of the anchor to 80% of its maximum and 10 degrees reduces it to 60%) and that the weight of the chain adds considerably to the holding power of the anchor as well as having a "spring effect". This is why rope — which is much lighter than chain — needs so much more scope, which is not always easy in a crowded anchorage or small harbour. Most full-time cruising folk curse boats lying to rope for the disproportionate size of their swinging circle and for the hazard their rope rodes present to yachts manoeuvring nearby.

If you must use the rope/chain combination (especially when lying stern- or bow-to a quay), lower a weight down the anchor cable on a messenger line to sink the cable below the surface. If you do not have a patent device (eg a "Chum") an old style 25 lb or even 50 lb (10-20 kg) cast iron weight will serve very well, or anything similar. If it is rust-prone, you can cover it with GRP cloth and resin to minimise the nuisance. Incidentally, you will also lie all the more comfortably as the weight will absorb a lot of surge. Make sure you have a chain claw or hook (see Chapter 10).

You will be anchoring far more than you are probably used to doing, so think hard about how you will lift "Old Coldnose" with a minimum of effort and how he can be made self-stowing if this is not already the case. Do have a windlass of some sort forward (see Chapter 6) and if it is a manual one, try for a two-speed type — 40 metres is one devil of a lot of chain to haul in, especially if you have to reset it two or three times and "Murphy" will see to it that you do! Think too about handling the brute from aft; you will

need to do so, especially if you adopt bow-in berthing. Perhaps you can mount a large two- or three-speed sheet winch aft: it doesn't have to be right aft — you can do a lot with a snatch block or two to obtain the right lead.

Such a winch will also earn its keep when you have to tension a long line to the shore: sometimes a necessary evil. Make sure your fairleads and bitts/cleats are up to the job: too often the standard ones fitted to production yachts are tiddly toys.

Bilge pump

It may seem pernickety to mention such an obvious item, but check your installation. If you have an electric one, fit it to an automatic float switch via a manual/auto switch. You also need a large capacity fully manual pump — an old-fashioned semi-rotary one will be fine — for emergency use. You can bet your life the electric one will burn-out or the batteries go flat just when you need it most. Ours went unserviceable during a gale in the Gulf of Suez and we blessed the "up and down" hand pump though it was hard work pumping on the side deck with green water coming on board. Better siting would have alleviated this, so give some thought to the siting of the manual pump. A spare cheap electric pump is probably worth carrying. Make sure you have a good "strum box" on the bilge end of the pipe.

Oh! We assume you have an echo sounder (and a leadline, again to foil "Murphy"!).

Water

We would recommend that you have capacity for about 200

gallons (900 litres). Fit further tankage if necessary. The problem is not always the distance between available supplies but the distance between supplies of drinkable water. Always taste the water before filling your tanks. At one port we narrowly escaped topping up our supply with undrinkably brackish (almost salt) water. We were saved from this fate by having a shower ashore before we tackled the water job: Bill was thoroughly soaped-up when the water ran very salty, leaving him most uncomfortable and sticky until he was able to have a shower at a later port! It did, however, lead us to taste (and reject) the water on offer on the pontoons.

Fit a good bacteriological and biological filter (e.g. a silver and carbon impregnated filter such as a Stockdale or Aquacity) to one tap which can then be used for drinking purposes. (Again, don't forget spare filter cartridges). You can use bottled waters for drinking purposes if you are doubtful about the local supply. We saw one particularly apprehensive crew buy 400 x 1.5 litre bottles of spa water, have the supplier deliver it and then make the poor guy pour it, bottle by bottle, into their tank!

You will almost certainly have an electric pressure water system — but don't forget to have a manual draw-off pump or point in case the electric system fails. Carry spares for the pressure pump, e.g. pulsation dampeners, diaphragms, drive belt, valves and maybe a pressure switch. Plumb the supply to wash-hand basin(s) and the shower as well as to the galley if this is not already done.

For hot water, use a gas-fired 'on demand' water heater (eg. Calor, Vaillant, Bosch etc.) and/or use a storage tank with water heated by a heat-exchanger system from the main engine. Duplicate the cold water plumbing for the hot water. Solar-heated bags are good for sluicing-off after swimming and even for a "cleansing shower" in the right time and place; moreover they are very economical with water. Be careful — they can become very hot.

Have a salt-water supply point at the galley — either a hand or foot pump or a simply switched electric system: for example a Jabsco "Water Puppy" pump drawing from one of the salt-water inlets is effective and pretty foolproof. Suitable use of salt water (obviously not in harbour!) can eke out the fresh-water supply nicely.

Carry a hose at least 60 ft (20 m) long with assorted fittings for the shore end — you will inevitably have to acquire more en route! We recommend "heavy" reinforced hose rather than the more convenient fold-flat types which won't stand up to the heavy use you will give them. Having said that, a "fold-flat" hose is useful to have on board to extend the standard hose when the latter is not long enough.

Electricity

You will already have a D.C. system installed but you will find it extremely helpful to make a circuit diagram of it and whenever convenient (e.g. when you are tracing a line) to number both ends of the cables with the clip-on or stick-on letters/numbers sold in good electrical shops for the purpose. We didn't realise how useful a circuit diagram was until we 'inherited' one.

Think about battery charging systems. If it is not already the case, have separate engine starting and service banks, each monitored by its own battery-state meter. By all means have a change-over switch for emergency use but make a practice of not using the engine-starting bank for domestic use. Check the engine alternator capacity: not only will you be making much heavier use of the service batteries than with normal weekend sailing but you will probably add more equipment too. It may be wise to fit a larger alternator.

It is generally held to be better to switch charging manually between the engine and service battery banks: this is more reliable and loses less power than do splitting diodes. There are now "battery management systems" on the market which sound good. They use electronic technology and are worthwhile looking into if you can afford one though we have no experience to guide you.

Are your batteries in good condition and of sufficient capacity? If in doubt, renew them before sailing — you will probably buy better in your home port where you know your way around. For the service batteries, you will really need ones capable of frequently suffering deep discharge without damage. Normal car or truck starting batteries cannot take much of this treatment and there are batteries available with these attributes. The best, we are reliably told, are the batteries used on golf buggies: more expensive initially but much more reliable and cheaper in the long run.

You will need a battery charging system for maintaining your banks when lying at anchor as well as in port. At anchor you can use your main engine if necessary but battery charging is not really a sufficient load to be good for the engine. Seriously consider buying one of the compact portable generators now available such as a Honda, Mase or Kawasaki. These will also give you some A.C. power for portable tools and so on. It is possible to get sound-proofing boxes for some of them if you are sensitive to the noise.

You might like to look into solar panels and wind-powered generators, though to our mind it is debatable how worthwhile they are. It depends on how much gear you have to support. On the face of it, solar panels have everything going for them. They are ecologically harmless, they need no maintenance, they are silent, they use free energy from the sun and they are long-lasting. Unfortunately they are relatively expensive, difficult to site satisfactorily and have a very small output which is only fully realised when the sun is shining on them. For a boat that sits unused in a marina all week, a solar panel system can keep a useful trickle charge running into the batteries. For a yacht in daily use, however, one has to calculate the ampere/hours regularly used by her gear to determine if a solar panel source will be sufficiently significant to justify its fitting.

To be most effective the sun's rays should strike the panel at right-angles; shadows adversely affect output as does poor alignment with the sun and — surprisingly —

high temperatures. A high-efficiency panel measuring 22 x 13 in (570 x 330 mm) which receives six hours of well-directed sunlight should produce about 7 A/Hrs at 14 volts.

Flexible panels are now available: these can, for example, be fitted to semi-permanent cockpit pram-hoods, Bimini covers etc. provided they do not suffer much shading from sails, for instance. A typical, good quality flexible panel measuring about 27 x 15 in (690 x 395 mm) should, in the same conditions, generate about 4.2 A/Hrs at 14 volts. Several panels can, of course, be linked together if space permits — although it rarely does.

Rigid panels should not be walked upon, a restriction which technically does not apply to the flexible ones although it is not to be recommended as, in time, their surface would become scratched thus diminishing their efficiency.

Wind generators are really in a different category. Typically, one might expect a six-bladed version, 39 in (1 m) across the blades, to produce about 4 amps at 14 volts in a wind speed of 14 knots or so. As they are independent of sunlight, they will produce electricity for 24 hours a day if the wind is blowing.

Leaving aside these possible sources of power, you will need a good marine battery charger to hook up to the mains supply in port (e.g. Constavolt, Cetrek, Professional Mariner). Don't forget to take plenty of battery water: buy a

BELOW *A swing-mounted solar panel which can be moved to follow the sun.*

BELOW *A wind-driven generator could be a good investment.*

couple of 5 pint (2.5 litre) bottles rather than a number of fancy (and pricey) smaller ones. If you are not very knowledgeable about D.C. circuits, buy a good book on the subject. We shall deal with fitted generators in Chapter 6.

It is well worth fitting an A.C. ring main for use when you are in a port with A.C. power available. Use a proper waterproof intake plug and socket for receiving the supply from the shore. You will need a variety of plugs to fit the shore supply points but you can collect these as necessary en route. Use a heavy gauge shore lead to minimise the voltage drop, and we would recommend routing both the line and neutral leads via 35-40 amp circuit breakers between the inboard socket and the switchboard. If your home country supply is 110v A.C., fit a switchable step-down transformer to cater for 240v systems. Similarly, if your usual supply is 240v and you are visiting 110v territory, have a suitable step-up transformer. Note that the 50:60 Hz difference will affect some but by no means all equipment; keep this in mind when buying and seek advice.

Run as many ring circuits as convenient but keep the power and lighting circuits separate. Separately switch each ring via appropriately rated circuit breakers as well as the normal switches on the lights and sockets. If in doubt, have the installation purpose-designed and professionally checked after installation, or have it professionally fitted in entirety. Keep a circuit diagram. Fit an ammeter on the inward line to monitor the current drawn: shore supply capacity varies widely from less than 5 amps to 30-plus amps. We shall deal with alternative sources of A.C. power under the "nice to haves" section in Chapter 6.

Cooking and heating

Chapter 8 deals with galley fittings but here we shall consider fuel types. You can choose between butane/propane gas, kerosene, gas oil and alcohol. (A.C. for cooking needs a built-in generator — see Chapter 6). Alcohol of an acceptable grade is not always easy to obtain. Gas oil is inclined to be rather dirty/smelly for cooking. Kerosene is widely available but its cleanliness varies a lot. We would go for gas every time — with suitable precautions.

Stow gas bottles on deck or in a locker which drains overboard. Fit a gas detector with sensors under the appliances and in the bilge (e.g. Thos. Walker, Simpson-Lawrence, Plastimo, Xintex etc). Fit a remote solenoid switch operated both automatically by the detector and manually by a switch in the galley. Switch off the supply at the bottle via the manual switch when the gas is not in use. With these precautions gas should be as safe or even safer than oil.

Gas is readily available: Camping Gaz is available throughout Europe but is frequently very expensive and the largest bottle available is inconveniently small. It is possible, practical and much cheaper to use the brands obtainable in each country. The deposit on the bottle(s) is refundable on departure; you may have to buy the valves but often these are common between countries. Have (say) two Camping Gaz bottles as reserves to see you from one country to another.

If you have some "expatriate" bottles (eg. with which you left your home port) it is often quite easy to get them refilled but the filling stations are not always conveniently sited. Also, the stations may not have fittings to fit your bottles so make the effort to obtain such fittings — with an on/off tap but no reduction valve — for refilling purposes.

You may think it strange to refer to heating when your whole aim is to live in a warmer climate but it can be cool even in the tropics. You may also need to dry out the boat in prolonged wet weather. Heating options are gas fires; catalytic heaters using gas, kerosene or oil; blown warm air; a closed or open stove using gas, oil, charcoal and sometimes coal or wood and (when on shore power) fan heaters.

Any flame device will produce some condensation unless it is vented. This is not necessarily serious and certainly not serious enough to prevent their use. The gas options are probably the cheapest and, provided they are used carefully, are safe. The gas fires with integral cylinders are highly effective and mobile but they are difficult to stow when not required. The stove designs generally require bulkhead space and need a chimney to the deck. They are quite effective for small areas (e.g. Taylor, Force 10, Dickinson etc). Probably best, in our view, are blown air systems using a gas-oil fired ducted furnace and a D.C. electric circulating fan. These can have several outlets and be connected to a thermostat, and the furnace unit is compact enough to be fitted into a small space (e.g. Eberspatcher).

5 GETTING HER READY
More essentials

- Warps and fenders
- Tender
- Safety equipment
- Passerelle and boarding ladder
- Refrigeration

Warps and fenders

Have enough good warps to make fast alongside in the traditional manner: head and stern ropes, two breast ropes and two springs. On occasion, you will have to raft and if lying offside you will need longish ropes to reach the shore from bow and stern. It is not always possible for offside boats to get head and stern lines ashore (even if the lines they have are long enough and you manage to persuade them to try) so your lines may have to hold three or four other yachts. Don't imagine that all folk who take to the sea are seamen...

We shall deviate for a moment to recount an unbelievable story — but it's true, honestly! A few yachts were in a quiet Greek harbour when a middling-sized gin-palace entered and, ignoring the fact that everyone else was berthed bow- or stern-to, proceeded to go alongside. Those on board wasted no time in getting ashore and adjourning to their chosen taverna. After a short time, the yachties noticed that the motor yacht appeared to be drifting off and upon investigation they could find no sign of any mooring lines. Naturally, after scratching their heads briefly, they made the errant boat fast. When her "crew" returned, replete with ouzo and kebabs, they were quizzed as to why had they not moored their boat to the quay? They were

BELOW *It is often necessary to 'raft off'; if you are one of the outer yachts you will need very long lines to reach the shore.*

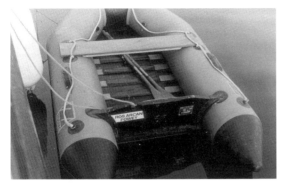

ABOVE *Mark your dinghy clearly with the ship's name. It might deter a thief and certainly saves confusion.*

somewhat puzzled at the implied criticism. 'What was wrong?' they enquired, 'we left her in gear!'

Also have at least one very long medium weight line — preferably at least 150 ft (45 m) long — for making the stern fast to the shore when anchored (this is sometimes unavoidable) or, when moored stern-to, to hold your bow against a strong beam wind. The need to lie to anchor ahead and shore-line astern is unfortunately occasionally necessary in crowded anchorages. There is no objection on our part when the wind is from ahead or astern; the trouble arises when this is not the case and the beam wind freshens to put an unnatural strain on your gear. If you are fortunate the anchor won't drag but you will become increasingly uncomfortable about the stresses until, in the middle of the night, the chap to windward of you will drag and chaos ensue...

A long line from the bow to the quay when you are lying stern-to with a strong beam wind is not always possible, of course, but it is not the same thing as a stern line to the shore and is very welcome when it is feasible. We shall return to anchoring/mooring techniques in Chapter 10.

As to fenders, carry enough good ones adequately to protect both sides of your boat: regrettably many others either do not have enough or are too disinterested to use them. If your fenders are a conveniently portable size, mark them well as they may develop a tendency to 'go walkabout'. Small old tyres, each with a drain hole cut through the tread and wrapped in soft (eg. cotton) rope, or used bare with your topsides suitably protected by "curtains", are very handy — particularly if you have to lie against a rough wall. Unfortunately, tyres are a nuisance to stow. Two or three may become part of the deck cargo you'll end up carrying!

Tender

Try to have a reasonably-sized dinghy: you will use it a good deal for exploring and it will need to carry a decent load when you are not alongside and you have to use it for your shopping. Whatever kind of dinghy you have, mark it clearly and as permanently as possible with the ship's name.

Some rigid dinghies are seen but most boats carry an inflatable. This is very often carried in the inflated state as it is used so frequently, so a convenient stowage has to be devised unless the dinghy is towed astern which is usual practice on short daily passages. Davits are commonplace and seem to be attractive until one is shipmates with them. We are by no means alone in getting rid of ours because of their nuisance value when making-up stern-to. Try manoeuvring stern-first into a tight space with a strong cross wind when your boathook won't stretch sufficiently beyond the davit-stowed dinghy! Davits can also inconveniently complicate the rigging of your passerelle, but everyone to his taste.

Some people carry the inflatable on its side across the transom: it seems to be fine in calm weather but to our mind is unseamanlike in its vulnerability and windage. We would rather tow, or if the weather or length of the passage is against towing, partly or totally deflate it and lash it firmly on deck as convenient.

An outboard could be termed an optional item rather than an essential, but there is no doubt that it is a useful member of the crew, particularly on a hot day with shops or whatever a long way off and maybe well upwind.

Safety equipment

We are assuming that you have a sensible complement of lifejackets and safety harnesses on board and that you have thought about how you would recover someone from overboard when you are short-handed. We are not going to discuss this difficult and often contentious problem — there are so many imponderables, and we don't believe there is any set routine that could be applied.

The only really sound advice is to take all sensible precautions against going over the side, including harnessing

ABOVE *This stanchion foot straddles the toerail and is bolted through for strength. Note also the strongpoint on the chainplate for lifting the yacht out of the water.*

ABOVE *An alternative arrangement with the stanchion foot bolted through the toerail. Notice the simple but effective fairlead for mooring lines.*

yourself to the boat while working on an open deck if there is any sort of sea running and always at night or when on watch alone. We strongly recommend having permanent jackstays rigged, in such a way that you are able to clip on the safety harness before leaving the security of the cockpit.

Further very desirable safety features are guardrails made as strong as you can: people will push you off by your stanchions which imposes an unnatural strain on them and can very quickly lead to their deck fastenings becoming insecure. Apart from politely asking the ignorant to desist from abusing your stanchions in this manner, the most positive thing you can do is examine their attachment method (odds-on you will be dissatisfied with it) and employ adequately-sized bolts through both toerail and deck with backing pads to spread the load.

You may not intend going far offshore but do not rely upon rescue services existing, arriving promptly or even turning out at all. For example, we know of one yacht that was precariously balanced on a rock off Majorca for five hours during the night. The crew called frequently on VHF Channel 16 for most of that time before the call was even acknowledged: fortunately it was a quiet, calm night. Therefore we recommend that you at least carry the safety equipment you would have on board if you were in an offshore race in your home waters. Unfortunately the equipment is expensive for something you hope you will never need to use, but if you do need it, then its value is

beyond price. Apart from this, some countries have the right to inspect your boat and to hold you until they are satisfied that you are adequately equipped; they may even fine you.

Fire extinguishers Do have sufficient fire extinguishers of appropriate types positioned tactically throughout the ship. There are three basic types of fire that you might be unlucky enough to encounter on board:

1 Straight-forward combustible materials such as wood, paper, cloth, some (but not all) plastics and so on.
2 Flammable liquids such as petrol (gasoline), diesel (gas) oil, paraffin (kerosene), alcohol, lubricating oil, paints. and white spirit
3 "Live" electrical fires which can include burning insulation on or near live wires and fires kept burning by arcing.

There are, in essence, five different extinguishing agents:

• **Water** — advantages are that it is relatively clean, is non-toxic and is usually available in quantity! Its disadvantages include its unsuitability for use on fires in categories 2 and 3 above.
• **"Regular" dry powder** (sodium bicarbonate) — has the advantage of being fairly inexpensive and non-toxic, but

it is ineffective on category 1 fires.

- **Tri-class dry powder** (mono-ammonium phosphate) — is also relatively inexpensive and non-toxic. Moreover, it is effective on all three types of fire.
- **Carbon dioxide** — is effective on categories 2 and 3, but less effective on category 1. Being a gas, there is no cleaning-up aggravation, but it is ineffective except in enclosed places. It does, of course, contribute to the "greenhouse effect" and an ozone-friendly alternative will no doubt appear.
- **Halon** (BCF) — is effective on all types of fire listed above and causes very little mess. It is also effective in much larger spaces than is carbon dioxide (unless there is a strong wind, of course) though it too is a "greenhouse" gas and will probably be phased out in favour of a more ecologically-acceptable alternative.

We would therefore recommend that you have one 2.5 lb. (1 kg) tri-class powder extinguisher in each "living" compartment and in the cockpit. In the engine compartment, you should consider having an automatically triggered halon extinguisher of a capacity sufficient to deal with the cubic volume of the compartment. One further halon or carbon dioxide extinguisher of about 2.5 lb.(1 kg) in the cockpit for use anywhere on the ship might be a good idea.

Buy reputable makes and check them annually. Such checking consists of visual external inspection, weighing of gas extinguishers (some have a pressure gauge which confirms their contents) and the emptying of the powder from a dry extinguisher to weigh the gas cartridge and ensure the powder is dry and loose. Be careful when emptying out the powder — it is so fine it blows everywhere if there is the slightest wind!

You may think we have been pretty generous with our fire extinguisher complement but a fire on board is a very serious matter indeed and you have to deal with it quickly and effectively if you are to save your ship — and your lives!

Radar reflector Fit a good radar reflector such as a Firdell. We would recommend that you fix it permanently to a mast which is not difficult and infinitely better than rigging it when you feel it is necessary or having it swinging from a halyard. If you use one of the older octahedral types of reflector, be sure to mount it in the correct "rain catching" position: we can say from our own experience when using radar that the echo from an incorrectly-mounted one is minimal.

Flares Leave your home port with an adequate set having full or near-full life in hand. It is often difficult to obtain new ones (even expensively) and they are not something one can carry back by air after a trip home. A Verey pistol is perhaps an embarrassment as some places (including the UK) consider it to be a firearm.

Liferaft In our view a liferaft is an essential and it is not wise to buy the cheapest. Have a full survival kit in the liferaft; remember the possibility of delayed rescue. Have it properly inspected at the recommended intervals — sun and salt water can be insidious and will quickly ruin a good liferaft if not caught in time, even one in a canister. Try to see your raft unpacked — it is not only interesting and instructive but it also ensures the raft is serviced! We are well aware that inspection is an expensive affair but without it you have no idea if the raft will work if you have to pull the cord. You might just as well have a cardboard cut-out as an unreliable raft!

Lifebelts You should have a minimum of two, at least one of which should be equipped with an automatic floating light (eg.McMurdo, ACR, Forespar), a small drogue and a whistle. They should be within easy reach of the helmsman and not lashed down, since if they are needed you will need them in a hurry.

There is a lot to be said for a Dan Buoy, with or without an automatic light. A good throwing line with a quoit is an inexpensive but sensible thing to carry. A floating orange smoke signal stowed handily could lead you back to someone overboard. Check (if you don't already know) if your Maritime Administration has a minimum safety specification, and that you meet (if not exceed) it.

An EPIRB (Emergency Position Indicating Radio Beacon) is expensive but recommended if you are going offshore (e.g. to islands involving a passage of say 300 miles or more). You take it with you if you have to abandon ship. A hand-held VHF set is also an invaluable safety item, but see Chapter 6.

ABOVE *A folding aluminium passerelle with wheels on the shore-end,
raised clear of the quay by wrapping the lifts around the ends.*
ABOVE RIGHT *A home-made wooden passerelle, showing the fitting
that allows it to swivel horizontally and vertically on the stemhead.*
RIGHT *A simple wooden passerelle.*

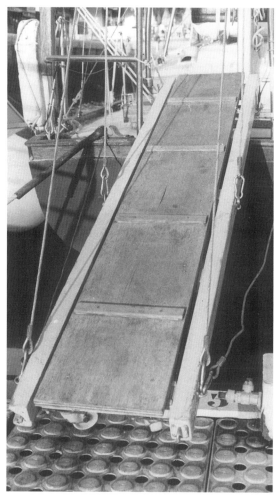

Panic bag Have a bag (if possible one which will float)
readily to hand containing useful items in addition to those
packed in the liferaft — e.g. an extra knife, a can-opener,
three or four tins of high-protein food, any medicines
frequently used by one or other of the crew, chocolate, sun
block, two foil blankets, photocopies of the ship's papers,
passports, insurance policy and any other important
papers.

Navigation lights Finally, but not to be forgotten, use an
approved make of navigation lights (eg.Aqua Signal)
mounted in accordance with the collision regulations and
correctly used. It is extraordinary how many unnecessary
and confusing displays of lights one sees (and how many
small vessels don't show any lights at all!).

Passerelle and boarding ladder
A passerelle (or gangway) of some sort is virtually essential:
one does see folk scrambling over the pulpit having pulled
their ship as close to the quay as they can, but why make
life difficult? It can be a simple wooden plank if necessary
or a more professional aluminium gangway. You can buy
ready-made aluminium ones ranging from cheap to

expensive but it is not difficult to make your own based on an aluminium ladder.

You need a fairly strong aluminium ladder of appropriate length — six feet (two metres) or more — to which you attach a pair of plastic wheels (straight or on castors) at one end and some suitable fitting of your own devising to fasten to the boat at the other. You then fasten a piece of marine grade plywood to the rungs, fitting it inside the sides of the ladder and hey presto! — a passerelle.

You will also need some form of boarding ladder for getting back on board from the dinghy (unless you are pretty athletic — but remember your guests) and to climb out of the sea after bathing. If you have a modern yacht with a bathing platform built into her transom, you have no problem as a bathing/boarding ladder will be there already. However, if you board from the ship's side, you will have to devise something suitable.

This is really a matter of using your ingenuity. You will probably already have a ladder of some sort for use with the dinghy, so maybe you can devise an easily-fixed extension to go into the water for bathers (and possibly to assist in recovery of a man overboard). One of the available types of folding aluminium ladder may be suitable or adaptable, or you can make up an extension from two pieces of wood or stainless steel tubing with wooden steps

BELOW *A substantial wooden boarding ladder with a removable stainless steel extension .*

A HOME-MADE PASSERELLE

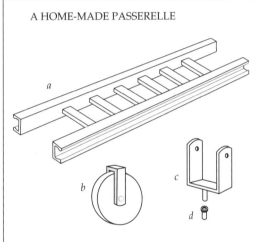

a. Aluminium ladder of required length and strength. Try to get one with square rungs.
b. A plastic wheel with alloy fixing obtainable from hardware stores.
c. Bracket to fit
d. Socket which can be made up for the inboard end. The socket can be let into the aft rail or modified to bolt to the transom.

The ladder should be fitted with decking of 12mm marine plywood, fastened to the ladder by self-tapping screws. It can be painted with deck paint, have non-slip strip applied to it or have wooden strips screwed across it. The wheels can be attached with pop rivets, bolts, or self-tapping screws. Optional stanchions are a straight-forward addition. The shore ends should have an eyebolt at each end to take lifts and guys to control the passerelle.

bolted across them. There is a great deal to be said for a rigid extension into the water — it need only have two or three rungs immersed. A "floppy" rope or folding plastic ladder is difficult for many people to use because the ladder pushes away from you under the boat as you put your weight on it.

Refrigeration

We don't entirely agree between ourselves whether this falls into the "essential" or "nice-to-have" category so it is at the end of the "essentials" section. You can get by without a fridge but this increases your reliance on tinned goods and/or very frequent shopping. It is also very nice to be able to have cool drinks.

At a pinch you can make do with an ice box — in marinas and fishing ports you can usually buy ice blocks or crushed ice — but this does increase your reliance on harbours rather than anchorages. You can make your own chiller/freezer lockers either by converting suitable existing lockers or by building-in new ones. Kits are available to make and inject insulation foam and you line the inside of your chosen compartment with plastic laminate (e.g. Formica) or stainless steel. Read up on the subject and consult good chandlers.

If you are going for refrigeration, try very hard to have both freezer and chiller lockers. Thoroughly investigate the market for the machinery: the eutectic plate system is unarguably the best to have at present, but technology moves so fast that by the time you read this there may be a better method.

Simply stated, the eutectic plate is a sort of "radiator" filled with a heat (or rather cold) retaining fluid such as glycol. A power source (the engine or an electric motor) drives the evaporator to chill down the fluid in an hour or two each day and the fluid then retains its freezing temperature for a considerable time — well in excess of twelve hours is not unusual — so holding the locker at cold

to freezing temperatures. You can, if running the cooling machinery from electric power, connect it to a thermostat. Otherwise, you simply keep an eye on the temperatures in the various lockers and provide cooling power when you consider it desirable.

As mentioned, the power supply can be from the engine or service batteries. Engine-driven systems are popular as there are few days when the engine is not run enough — for propulsion — to re-cool the fridge system. This does mean, of course, that unless you install an alternative electric power source, you will have to run your engine for an hour or two each day even when you are moored up in port. The vital thing to remember is the absolute requirement for really good insulation so don't skimp it.

Avoid D.C. motor compressors if possible — they are very demanding on batteries. Gas operated fridges are good and are fairly economical but they probably won't work at a sustained angle of heel of much over 10 degrees which rather negates their value if you are having a really good sail on the wind. We have a small Camping Gaz "Groenland" chest refrigerator which is used only for drinks. It makes two trays of ice, works on 12v D.C. (which we never use), on 220v A.C. and on gas. It has given several years of excellent service even though it is stowed on deck.

Leading suppliers from whom fully descriptive literature is available are Danfoss, Frigoboat, Thermocool etc. The stock yacht refrigerators (eg. Engel, Electrolux, LVM, Norcold etc.) can be satisfactory but are of varying efficiency and typically can draw 5-6 amps at 12v which is a heavy load for your batteries. As mentioned above, whichever system you adopt, try to have a machine which will work off A.C. power as well as other sources to make life easy when lying alongside with power laid on. You will not want to run your main engine every day and if you are on the "hard" you cannot do so anyway.

6 OPTIONAL EXTRAS
The 'nice to haves'

- **Autopilot**
- **Electronic navigation aids**
- **Electric windlass (anchor winch)**
- **Radio**
- **Radar**
- **Built-in generator**
- **Fresh water maker**
- **The toybox**

We weren't there at the time but are reliably told that, in the first century A.D., Pliny the Elder said words to the effect that 'as with a woman, there is no limit to how much a man can spend on cosmetics and adornments for his ship!' So what is new? Thus we now turn to some of the other items of gear that are nice to have if you can afford them and which are (in all or part) regularly seen on board full-time cruising yachts. The Larnaca survey sheds some interesting light on these. The following list of gear and the percentages of yachts carrying it is very revealing:

Autopilot	91.3%
Inflatable dinghy	89.1%
Hard dinghy	21.7%
(some had both inflatable and hard dinghies)	
VHF	86.9%
(32.6% also had a portable VHF)	
Refrigerator	84.7%
(23.9% also had a deep-freezer)	
Headsail furling	71.4%
Satnav	67.3%
Electric (or hydraulic) anchor windlass	62.7%
Portable generator	43.4%
Wind vane	39.1%
"Ham" radio	39.1%
Radar	34.7%
Navtex	32.6%
Solar panels (71 watts average)	28.2%
Built-in generator	28.2%

Wind powered generator	17.3%
Loran C	15.2%
Weatherfax facility	15.2%
Fresh water maker	6.5%

And what did our fellow 'live-aboards' have on their shopping lists? In percentage terms of those surveyed, the following gear featured:

Radar	36.9%
In-mast mainsail furling	28.2%
(no one actually had it so there was no experience to draw upon)	
Fresh water maker	23.9%
Solar panels	17.3%
"Ham" radio	15.2%
Built-in generator	13.0%
Electric anchor windlass	8.6%
Loran C	6.5%
Deep-freezer	4.3%

We have already commented on dinghies, refrigeration, furling headsails, portable generators, solar panels and wind-powered generators in Chapters 4 and 5. We shall now have a look at the others items listed above as well as at some gear which was not included in the Larnaca census.

Autopilot

By the percentage of yachts already having one on board, perhaps an autopilot should have been on the "essentials" list. The undeniable fact is that modern autopilots draw so little current and are so efficient that they can take a great deal of the strain out of passage-making whether under sail or power. Your object is to enjoy yourselves; you can always switch off the autopilot if you want to take the helm yourself but it's nice to have one when the sailing is lacking sparkle, when you are motoring or when you are getting tired and stiff. It is a godsend to relieve the night watch-keeper on that long, dark or shirty night. The Larnaca yachties rated their performance factors highly too.

Electronic navigation aids

We much prefer to talk of navigation *aids* as none of this electronic wizardry should seduce you into forgetting your manual skills (or not bothering to acquire them in the first place). One of Bill's former navigation lecturers — the delightfully crusty Cmdr. Rantzen — used to refer to "the days before education took over from common-sense"; well, there is a place for a variant on his salty comment relevant to electronics! But microchip-wizardry is here and it is certainly "nice to have".

Bear in mind, when looking through the catalogues, the broad generalisation that you get what you pay for. We very deliberately say "broad" as there comes a stage when the extra expenditure merely provides more gimmicks which — having tried for the fun of it — you will rarely if ever use in practice. We suggest that you identify what you expect the magic box to give you and then try to ascertain its "user-friendliness" as the jargon has it. Only then, short-list the possibles.

One point we would suggest you don't overlook is the instrument's capability to "interface" with other equipment. Maybe at present you have no intention of linking in one instrument with another, but there may come a time when you invest in something else and find that a simple cable is all that's required to have the two boxes communicating with each other to your further advantage. Generally, all you have to look for is the statement that your proposed purchase will provide a "NMEA 0183 output". So, let's look at:

Satnav Frankly, unless you can pick up a set very cheaply, there is now little point in considering the Transit system. It will be around for only a few years to come and when compared to the GPS system it is distinctly "steam driven". The cost of GPS receivers in the UK has already fallen to below £650 (and they are cheaper in the US). Prices will undoubtedly fall further in the next year or two and the system, with its remarkable accuracy and virtually instantaneous fixes, makes it a coastal as well as an off-shore navigation aid of a very high order.

Whether or not GPS renders Decca or Loran C totally redundant we cannot yet judge: its service reliability has perhaps to be proved and its vulnerability to 'political' (ie military) interruption is still uncertain. However, much the same arguments could have been put forward about the Transit system.

Conclusion: if you want Satnav go for GPS but bear in mind that the former USSR has its own version of GPS which will presumably continue to operate and may become commercially available and very competitive. It is your guess what may arise from having competing systems...

Loran C Very cheap Loran receivers can now be obtained, at half or less of the current price of the cheapest GPS receiver. Loran's accuracy is not as high as that of GPS and the fix it gives you may be up to one-and-a-half miles out. Its areas of availability also need to be checked against your proposed cruising area(s).

At the time of writing, Loran C covers the east and west coasts of Canada and the USA, the Great Lakes, Iceland and Norway (including the UK and Ireland as far south as a line joining the River Humber to the Bristol Channel), the Mediterranean as far west as the Franco-Spanish border and east to Rhodes and the west Turkish coast, the Red Sea, Arabian Gulf and Mediterranean westwards to Cyprus (in practice overlapping the Rhodes coverage), Japan and adjacent seas and the US central Pacific territories. Although the northern Europeans have decided to continue to support the Decca chain, it is (at the time of writing) expected that the north-west European Loran C chain will go ahead and Loran signals of acceptable quality can already be received in the Biscay and English Channel areas.

If shopping for a Loran C receiver, bear in mind that the cheaper ones may not have the full range of 'notch filters' guaranteeing good reception in all areas. This is not necessarily a killer — if the area you propose to cruise is covered there is no problem and most sets (but not all) can have their filters re-tuned if you decide to sail on elsewhere. Check before buying.

Decca Broadly this works on similar lines to Loran C but it has a shorter range and generally greater accuracy. It serves all the north-west Atlantic, the Baltic, the North and Irish Seas, the English Channel and approaches up to 250-400 miles from the coast. The French transmitter has been closed down unilaterally leaving a gap in Biscay before the Spanish chain is picked up. As far as is currently known to the authors, Decca is also operative in parts of Australia, the Persian Gulf, Pakistan, India, Bangladesh, Japan, Canada and southern Africa.

So, do you go for Loran C and/or Decca? Loran C will not be supported by the US Government once GPS is fully operational and the USA proposes to sell the transmitting stations to their "host" countries. Most are expected to transfer accordingly so that there is not total reliance on GPS: thus preservation of Loran C chains may be anticipated. Indeed, there are signs that the system will spread. Decca, on the other hand, is probably dying as many stations are due for expensive equipment renewal. We would say only go for Decca after careful enquiry locally about its future.

RDF Although a number of Radio Direction Finding stations have been (or are scheduled to be) closed, it remains a useful position finding system in many parts of the world. (Not having Satnav at the time, we found it very useful in the Black Sea.) Moreover, a good hand-held RDF receiver comes with a high-quality hand-bearing compass which need be the only one you have to carry. Thus, in our view, an RDF receiver is an excellent and simple stand-by instrument to cover failure of Satnav, Loran or Decca.

Electric Windlass (anchor winch)

We referred in Chapter 5 to the desirability of a windlass. You will have noted the high proportion of electric windlasses carried by the Larnaca fleet: this is no accident. On a hot day the effort of hand-cranking your anchor from the deep (and maybe finding you are foul of someone else's chain — see Chapter 10) can take the gilt off the gingerbread to say the least.

There are a number of fairly compact and lightweight models on the market including the relatively new vertical ones (e.g. Lofrans, Simpson-Lawrence, Maxwell, Powerwinch etc.) We wonder why hydraulic windlasses are not more readily available — with small-bore piping now generally in use, its installation is much simplified and, if one has to run the main engine anyway to support a high consumption electric motor....

Although it may not be quite so compact, we prefer a horizontal windlass to a vertical one. If possible, have a

gypsy (wildcat) which can be operated separately from the rope drum — these are much more versatile than the combined type. A portable hand switch is probably better than a flush deck-fitted foot button: not only does it give the operator freedom to look over either bow when weighing anchor but a socket is easier to protect from salt-water ingress than a rubber-covered foot-operated button.

You will soon find the advantages of using the rope drum as a warping drum for hauling alongside or — with the assistance of suitably placed snatch blocks — for lifting weights such as the skipper up the mast! The lead for tailing a rope coming off a vertical drum is difficult being low to the deck (snatch blocks can eliminate this snag but involve further complicating problems).

Try to afford a reversible windlass with an extra solenoid switch for lowering away as well as hauling in. If such a windlass is also operable from the steering position it is a great help when berthing short-handed as it allows the second crew to attend to the after lines while the helmsman manoeuvres and lets out more chain as required. Most manufacturers market reversible models and their small additional cost is money well spent. Some manufacturers sell a special reversible control box which is a very convenient unit.

TOP LEFT *A vertical electric windlass of a good design, with a very useful rope drum.*

TOP *A horizontal electric windlass, well-mounted on the foredeck.* ABOVE *A horizontal rope drum is more versatile than a vertical one, and easier to tail.*

Bear in mind that an electric windlass will draw from 50 to 80 amps for up to five minutes at a time so you need plenty of battery power. You will also need to run the main engine alternator when operating it. The windlass must also be capable of being hand-cranked both in case of electrical breakdown and to lift a fouled anchor if the load is straining the electrics. Most electrically-powered windlasses have a motor rated at about 1000 watts and it is good practice to put a circuit breaker of 70-80 amps into the line as a safeguard against electrical overload.

Radio

We have already mentioned VHF as a piece of safety equipment, which of course it is. On Ch.16 you can call for assistance from shore stations or — in many cruising grounds — from fellow seafarers. It is also used for inter-yacht communication when cruising in company and in some parts of the world for receiving weather forecasts and navigational information.

Remember that VHF is mainly a 'line of sight' system so don't expect an inter-ship range of much over 25 miles. Some shore stations have remarkably long ranges owing to the height of their aerials. We have frequently and clearly heard Haifa Radio when in Cyprus 100 miles away but then Haifa Radio's antennae are on the top of Mount Carmel!

Have a good set with all the International Channels; if in the US area your set should include the US channels. As with all electronics, we repeat the opinion we've already expressed: it's simply not worth economising as it's very much a case of getting what you pay for.

As shown in the Cyprus survey, many boats also carry a portable VHF set; useful for keeping in touch with the shore-party to call for transport back to the ship.

MF/HF sets are a matter of choice and funds: the prices have a big range. You will need a special licence to operate on these frequencies over and above the usual VHF licence. MF/HF sets (especially the latter) have a much longer range than VHF and can speak with shore stations over considerable distances depending on propagation conditions. This may allow you to make link telephone calls via a coast station in your own country which saves overseas telephone charges. However, coast station charges can also be high and as a generalisation, a telephone call over the international public system is cheaper. Some telephone companies have special billing arrangements for radio links which work out cheaper than the international "gold francs" system: see also Chapter 2.

With VHF only and with MF/HF you need to have both a ship as well as a personal licence, and an agent who will receive (and if necessary pay) accounts.

Amateur Radio ("Ham") is achieving growing popularity among cruising boats. "Amateur" should not be construed as meaning less proficient than "professional" — most Amateurs are highly qualified and very experienced — and to use the system you must have a licence issued by the relevant National Authority. Hams use different frequencies than professionals and their procedures differ

The great attraction of Ham radio is the wide interchange of news and information of value to cruisers, and the assistance and advice that can be called up from fellow yachties. There are established "Maritime Mobile Nets" operating at regular times in various parts of the world, each with volunteer "Controllers" who manage the traffic — making sure no-one hogs the schedule, arranging relays between stations that can't work each other directly, passing on messages and so on.

One of the longest-established Ham nets is the UK Maritime Mobile Net which operates on 14303.0 KHz. and

has daily schedules (skeds) at 0800Z and 1800Z. The morning sked is mainly for reporting positions, intentions etc. (thus informing all of one's peers where you are and to where you hope to go) with a little weather information. The evening sked is for the same purpose but its major feature is the truly excellent weather service which gives forecasts derived from various meteorological services and which covers the area from south-west Ireland around the European coasts through the Mediterranean to Port Said, and also Atlantic sea areas from the West Azores south to the South Canaries. This is a service which it is difficult to imagine being equalled by any R.T. station.

In addition, the Net Controllers will gladly pass on information from one yacht to another and "emergency messages" to relatives and/or authorities. Recently, as we write, the UK Maritime Net had the sad task of passing on news of a drifting yacht in the North Atlantic whose solo crew had apparently been lost overboard: she was found by another yacht which gave details to the Net Controller and thus via him to the various authorities.

The people who commit themselves to the Controllers' task day-in day-out are owed an immense debt of gratitude by the cruising community. We know that similar Nets operate elsewhere in the world — books are available which give details. But Amateur traffic is not limited to Maritime Mobile stations; with a licence one can work any Amateur station in the world, but not into public telephone systems. Communication times/frequencies (skeds) can be arranged between any Amateur stations for any time of day or night on appropriate frequencies provided they do not interfere with other stations already working the same frequency at the time.

One can, of course, have similar arrangements on the appropriate International Maritime Bands. The International Maritime system has internationally agreed calling frequencies, frequencies for emergencies, traffic lists, weather and navigational information etc.

Both Amateur and "official" classes of radio use single sideband transmissions (SSB), but whereas the 'professionals' use only the upper sideband, amateurs also use some lower sideband frequencies. The "jargon" used with the two systems differs too but that is an incidental...

You can buy combined transmitter/receivers to work either or both Maritime and Amateur bands. Ensure the set will handle upper and lower sidebands. Note that

VHF and MF/HF systems have nothing in common with Citizen's Band Radio. If you simply wish to listen to the professional and amateur radio broadcasts for weather information and so on, you can use a good portable receiver handling up to the 22MHz band. These should also handle normal broadcast stations: e.g. Sony ICF 20001D, Sangean ATS-803A and others.

A good SSB receiver can also be used to pick up Weatherfax signals — see later in this chapter. Additionally, weather and navigational information is broadcast over the Navtex system — an international system under the auspices of the International Maritime Organisation. It is intended in due course to cover all Navareas although unfortunately its implementation seems to be patchy and slow. Messages are broadcast on 518 KHz. to schedules (but with emergency messages and gale warnings on receipt) and are received on dedicated receivers which either print out the data or display it on a screen (e.g. Racal-Decca Lokata Navtex 1, NASA Navtex).

Radar

Until you have been shipmates with radar, you do not realise its true value. It is not simply a limited-vision collision avoidance system but a top-value navigational aid. With it you can pick up buoys, land etc. long before they are in visual range, use it to fix your position; to pick up unlit hazards such as fishing boats and unlit obstructions at night or in low visibility. The latest generation of sets can fix guard zones, track potential collision hazards and give compass bearings among other useful attributes. Radar is also one of the "magic boxes" which will accept an NMEA 0183 input to allow interfacing with, for instance, a GPS or Loran C receiver.

Typical power consumption is 50 watts, or about 4.5 amps. at 12 volts. This drops to 40 watts (3.5 amps.) on stand-by when the scanner is not rotating but the set is ready to resume full operation at the touch of a button.

Built-in generator

A built-in generator gives A.C. power whenever you need it and can therefore power a battery charger, microwave oven, galley equipment. T.V., electric tools and any other A.C. equipment within its power capacity. Provided you have suitable space it is a most useful (albeit not cheap) addition to the boat's equipment. There are now many more units on the market than the 'original' Onan and G & M models which, while good, are also expensive both initially and for spares. Check the market thoroughly. We have to say that, sadly and although we love its product dearly, we have had more maintenance problems with our 8 kw generator than with almost any other single piece of equipment — and we have many friends with similar experiences.

For an alternative A.C. power source for up to 3 kw, to power appliances such as galley equipment, electric tools, computers, T.V./V.C.R, cassette players, hair dryer and including the capacity to start inductive motors of up to 0.5 H.P., (e.g. pumps) consider a static inverter. The technology has improved dramatically in recent years and inverters are now small, efficient (up to 95%) and give a suitable waveform for virtually all electronics. One can buy models giving up to 3000 watts power for half-an-hour and slightly less continuously and incorporating an "intelligent" battery charger and battery safeguard devices (e.g. Heart Interface and PROwatt — both leading US manufacturers).

We have said before there is no such thing as a free lunch and this certainly applies with A.C. electrical power on board. You will need plenty of battery power as 1 amp at 220v from an inverter will draw roughly 20 amps of 12v D.C. input (with 110v equipment, the current drawn is twice that used for an identical appliance rated for 220v; remember the formula — Watts = Volts x Amps).

The obvious discipline is that you do not use hungry electric equipment for long, or you use it only while your main engine and its alternator are operating. Floating the load in this manner would be common practice on a motor yacht and allows the total battery capacity to be smaller than otherwise — provided you do not over-do things while lying at anchor without the main engine running. With a bit of planning, floating the load, even on a sailing yacht, presents little difficulty but the input demand does underline our earlier comments about the desirability of having ample battery capacity able to weather deep discharge.

Note that it is vital to follow the wiring instructions carefully to isolate the A.C. output from any other A.C. power source if you do not want an expensive burning smell.

You will not wish to incur the expense of acquiring an inverter that far exceeds your power requirement, so a brief description of how to calculate your A.C. needs may

ABOVE *A 600 watt Heart Interface inverter, shown with a wineglass for scale!*

ABOVE *A big 1800 watt Heart Interface inverter tucked neatly out of the way.*

not be out of place. You have to begin by estimating what appliances you will use and for how long. As a very simple example, you may decide that you will use a microwave oven for a total of 20 minutes in a day and that it consumes 1000 watts. You will also want a food processor for 5 minutes at 800 watts and a TV/VCR at 50 watts for three hours. (Remember, you switch appliances off as soon as you have finished with them and do not leave them running unused). Your total daily consumption will be:

microwave	1000w x .33hr	(20 mins)	334 watt/hrs
food processor	800w x .08hr	(5 mins)	64 watt/hrs
TV/VCR	50w x 3 hrs	(180 mins)	150 watt/hrs
Total per day			548 watt/hrs

If you divide the watt/hour drain by 10 (allowing for the slight inefficiency of the inverter we would suggest 10 rather than 12 on a 12v system) you would have to replace 55 ampere/ hours into your battery bank.

As to the size of inverter you would require for the example above, you could arrange that when the microwave oven is in use no other demand of consequence will be made of the inverter. The peak load will therefore never be much above 1000 watts so a 1100w or 1200w inverter will suffice.

The knowledgable folk reckon that you should have 20% of your inverter's wattage in ampere/hours of battery capacity. Thus a 1200 watt inverter will need a battery capacity of at least 250 A/H at 12v. We hope the above is not total gobbledegook!

At present, static inverters do not seem to be as readily available at competitive prices in Europe as in the USA and you might have to consider importing one. We cannot comment on the position elsewhere in the world. Rotary converters are generally not so efficient, are more cumbersome and are equally if not more expensive.

While on the subject of power, there are now very sophisticated power/battery control systems which manage the charging of and off-take from batteries so that loads are shed in a logically sequenced order to preserve the batteries and prevent over-discharge. The systems also float D.C. loads while concurrently charging batteries at an appropriate rate which reduces as the batteries approach their charged state. The top-range Heart Interface inverters have battery protection and controlled charging systems incorporated, but not the load shedding facility or ease of ascertaining battery drain and condition. Needless to say, these new systems operate from the on-board A.C. generator output as well as from the shore supply. Some of the Heart appliances sense when alternative A.C. power is on stream and switch automatically from supplying A.C. power to charging the batteries. If you are interested, consult a good electrical supplier (with cheque book in hand!). We have no first-hand experience of the new control equipment and no doubt the market has its usual selection of "bad" as well as of "good" buys.

Fresh water maker

A fresh water maker certainly adds a new dimension to life on board. It makes you even more independent of the shore and overcomes the oft-recurring problems of poor supply and quality. Again, technology is improving and prices are slowly falling.

There are two principles — reverse osmosis and distillation. Both need power and the latter also requires heat which can be obtained by tapping into the main engine's fresh-water cooling system. If you are seriously considering installing a water maker, investigate the market thoroughly and try to obtain personal reports on the efficacy of various models.

The toybox

We shall now take a look at some of the "toys" we all carry. It's very rare to find a boat without at least one bicycle on board and usually two. These are very useful when going shopping — particularly with a trolley as a trailer. Bicycles also let you see something of the countryside which adds immeasurably to the enjoyment. Obviously the folding types are best, particularly if they are made of alloy or stainless steel (e.g. Bickerton, Dahon etc.) but whatever you can afford and stow is worth having. Some boats even carry 49cc. motor scooters and these are becoming increasingly common.

Nowadays, many yachts carry one or two windsurfing boards for which deck stowage is necessary: they are often stowed on edge inside the shrouds. It is also usual to have on board snorkel and flipper sets for all the crew. A lot of people also have a scuba set, but this sometimes causes difficulties with authorities who are concerned about excessive spear-fishing and the removal of antiquities from the sea-bed. However, there can be no doubt as to the value of scuba gear if not improperly used — exploring reefs, cleaning the hull, freeing the anchor from a snag, clearing a rope or net from the propeller etc.

Laptop or notebook computers are now becoming very popular and are being carried by increasing numbers of boats. They are used for all the obvious purposes but they are also very useful for correspondence and particularly for the customary Christmas letter outlining the year's events which often has a large mailing list. You can also obtain a variety of navigational programs: for working out sights, for planet and star recognition, for obtaining astro and tidal information, and even "perpetual" nautical almanacs. A very useful program, for which a good SSB radio and a demodulator is required, allows the reception of Weatherfax charts. One can have a simple Weatherfax program or go up-market to receive satellite pictures, decode satellite news transmissions, convert into and out of morse code etc. In fact, computing has become an absorbing hobby for many cruising people and it is rare, for a "get-together" not to include a discussion on the subject.

TV (with a VCR) is also now carried by a large number of cruising yachts — there will be long nights when you will enjoy both even though you may have left home partly to avoid them! Bear in mind, if buying new equipment, to get multi-system sets — that is those which will receive the British, Continental and US systems. If you can find gear which will also receive the uniquely French system (some are available) then so much the better. You can opt for one of the patent mast-top multi-directional antennas or rig a conventional antenna from a halyard when you wish to view. It is commonplace for yachts temporarily to exchange videos and to invite neighbours on board to see a film.

Photography, sketching and painting (usually watercolours) also rank highly amongst the popular pastimes as well as sewing crafts (for men as well as women — macrame/knotting for example). Many people run classes during the off-season lay-by in various subjects including art, computing, bridge, morse, aerobics and so on: indeed the "lay-by" period can be a very sociable time. Bridge is a particularly popular game among live-aboards. If you don't play, don't be deterred from learning. There are of course the fanatics, but most people leave them to get on with it on their own. Most yachtie bridge is purely social fun and there is always someone to teach you. June hardly knew a spade from a club (a puppy's paw!) but now enjoys a game and holds her end happily. Watch out in anchorages for the LAMBS flag (Larnaca Amateur Maritime Bridge Society); it may now be seen worldwide and is an invitation to make your number for a game.

Carry fishing lines too; we rarely catch anything except tiddlers for the cat but other people land all sorts of succulent fish and really put us to shame! If you do have a hungry and impatient moggie to feed, a throw net will usually collect a supper or two of bream, mullet or other small harbour fish.

Buy an octopus hook — a large eight-branched hook with a big white or silver weight — add a string or two of aluminium foil as attraction and (though not obligatory) a small piece of raw meat, bacon rind or somesuch. Fasten the hook to a reasonably strong line — the beast can weigh 2 or 3 pounds (a kilo or more) — and dangle it down the face of a roughish quay, in amongst rocks and so on. If you are lucky a succulent octopus will grab it and you can haul it to the surface. Surprisingly the octopus is not likely to let go even if not actually hooked. It will wrap itself around your hand as you remove it but that presents no problem — forget Jules Verne and other fictional ideas of being drawn into the deep! Your only remaining problem is to despatch it. The experts put their fingers inside (being careful not to be bitten by its strong beak) and with a quick jerk pull out its 'innards'. We cheat and hurl it to the concrete which is pretty quick. You have to do this in any case to tenderise it — somewhere between 60 and 100 times according to its size. Use some force. Then, having done the hard work, you must decide which way to cook it. Boiled, baked or rubbed well with salt and barbecued, the choice is yours (see *The Beaufort Scale Cookbook*, also published by Fernhurst). Enjoy it: octopus is very good eating.

We try to engage in most of these sidelines but, truth to tell, there are never enough hours in the day and we cannot now imagine how we ever found time to earn a living ashore!

ABOVE *The LAMBS flag — the Larnaca Amateur Maritime Bridge Society.*

LIVING ABOARD
Your creature comforts

- Galley essentials
- Useful galley equipment
- Basic stores
- Shopping abroad
- Catering in hot climes
- Furnishings and linen
- Laundry
- Sewing repairs
- Garbage
- Medical
- Flies, bugs and creepy-crawlies
- Pets
- Deck life
- Guests and entertaining

Galley essentials

The galley is an important part of your boat and should be carefully considered. For convenience and safety it should be possible for the cook to stand in one place and be able to reach everything he/she needs without having to move far. This is necessary in heavy weather when the cook may well be strapped in for safety. If possible the galley should be situated near the cockpit hatchway, both for coolness and air, but also so that the cook will be able to join, at least in part, with the conversation in the cockpit. Unless the cook is within reasonable proximity of fresh air he/she could be stricken with seasickness or even, in hot places, with heat exhaustion.

The cooker should have a minimum of two burners (though three or four are much better), a grill and an oven. It doesn't have to be a yacht cooker — there are suitably small domestic ones available and these are usually cheaper. Gimballing is not essential provided the cooker has reasonable fiddles or some other securing method (e.g. expanding curtain wire but not the plastic-covered type).

The galley should have the usual safety features — including a crash bar and safety strap. A fire extinguisher and a fire blanket are essential for obvious reasons.

TOP *The galley sink area with tiled splashback and cork surface. Note the taps for drinking water and salt water.*

ABOVE *Sharp knives and other utensils securely stowed on the inside of a locker door in the galley.*

Fit secure shelves for commonly-needed items such as condiments, seasonings and spices if these are not already in situ. It is useful to have implements to hand but these should not be left hanging loosely. Sharp knives should be carried in secure slots, not loose in drawers.

If the fridge has an opening door, pack everything which is at all moist into very tight-fitting lidded boxes. Otherwise, in a seaway, you can be sure it will all tip out onto the floor, all the loose lids will fall off and there will be a glorious mess on the cabin sole. In fact, if the fridge has shelves with a wire rim across the width of the shelf (which we find is usually at the back for some reason) then turn the shelf and have the wire rim at the front. This helps retain the contents of the fridge until you have what you need and can shut the door again. We also fitted a safety line to the fridge and freezer doors from hook eyes on one side to small clam cleats on the other.

Stretch-rubber cord (shock cord) is very useful for anchoring items you like to have handy. For instance you could use it to fix your vacuum pump-action flask to a convenient bulkhead, with the base resting on a solid

BELOW Our pump-action vacuum flask secured in position ready for use at sea.

surface. That way you have a secured source of instant boiling water.

All food and implement lockers/drawers should fasten securely, otherwise you can be sure that all the bottles and jars will fall out and break! Remember this 'stew' of tomato sauce, mustard, pickles, honey, broken glass and other delights is always 'brewed' when the boat is rolling or pitching and cleaning it up is NOT a pleasant task.

It is well worth investing in some of the non-slip mats you can now buy: try to get the fairly heavy mats — they are considerably more expensive initially but they last, which the thin sheet doesn't It is also possible to buy fairly heavy non-slip material by the yard. See Appendix 1 for a suggested basic equipment list. (See also page 88 of *The Beaufort Scale Cookbook*, also published by Fernhurst.

Work surfaces should be waterproof and easily cleaned — such as laminated plastic (eg Formica) or sealed cork tiles. Splash-backs should be of laminated plastic or ceramic tiles. Avoid woodwork near the cooker or protect it against scorching.

The sink (a twin bowl is very nice if possible but alas there is rarely space) is better oblong or square if there is space (they have more capacity than round ones). Buy a plastic washing-up bowl to fit into your sink — they are endlessly useful. Fit hot, cold and filtered fresh water taps plus a salt water tap (see Chapter 3).

Clean sea water (obviously avoiding drawing it from harbours or polluted areas) is useful for many things. You can cook vegetables in a mixture of less than one quarter sea water to over three-quarters fresh. Don't use undiluted sea water: it is far too salty though you can use it to boil eggs or heat (opened) tins — usually three or four tins will fit in a fair-sized pan. Undiluted sea water is also useful for cleaning vegetables, for cleaning work surfaces and soaking washing up cloths as it kills germs — all this saves precious fresh water. If it is really clean it is also a good antiseptic for washing out wounds in an emergency.

Try to make the galley as attractive as possible since the cook often spends a great deal of time in it. Aim to keep it light and airy. Deal with steam if possible by having an opening window/port overhead or an extractor fan. Installing an oscillating fan to keep the cook cool is a great boon. As well as good daylight, bright D.C. and A.C. lighting is advisable; groping round in poor light in nasty weather is no fun and can be positively dangerous. If you have an A.C. ring main install several A.C. power sockets (away from the sink and taps); in this cook's opinion two is a minimum number.

Useful galley equipment

Much depends on whether or not you have A.C. power on board but do remember that you may well be at an off-season winter berth for 4-5 months each year where shorepower will probably be available. A mini food processor or small electric coffee grinder/blender is justifiable. The mini food processor in particular is neat and easy to stow.

If you have A.C. power on board plus space, a microwave oven is a godsend. It is possible to buy D.C. powered microwaves but they are very expensive. It would almost be worthwhile running an A.C. one off a portable generator if there is one on board. This depends on budget, space and how keen a cook you are! We inherited ours with our boat and now would not be without it. It is so useful, not only for cool cooking in hot climates and greatly reducing the time the cook slaves in the galley, but for a host of other little things — drying the herbs you find all over the Mediterranean region or heating up a quick cup of water (saves water and fuel) for a hot drink.

Other people swear by electric kettles, toasters and so on. We rather like our electric sandwich maker but the choice depends on your personal preference and on your power supply.

Basic stores

There is very little point in loading up with large quantities of basics unless you know that something is most unlikely to be available in your proposed cruising area. Some hard-to-find items are drinking chocolate and cocoa, marmalade, barley, Spam, English mustard, English custard powder, Bovril, Marmite, Vegemite, tinned mushrooms, and tinned ham (though ham and pork luncheon meat is fairly common). If you are visiting a Muslim country or Israel, there will be virtually no ham or pork products to be found. Cornflakes are normally available in most places but other breakfast cereals are much less likely to be freely available.

In addition there may be some ingredients which you use frequently but might not expect to find in New Guinea, the Lesser Antilles or Morocco — if so take them but ensure they will keep before you buy too much.

Generally speaking, the poorer the country the more basic will be the supplies, which is understandable. In the UK, Northern Europe, Gibraltar, Malta, Cyprus, Singapore, North America, Australia and New Zealand and like places you can buy virtually anything you will need.

Some things lose their potency with age, for instance common herbs and spices, but they are usually easily available anyway. Having generalised like this, we suggest you take some essential supplies in the dry goods line — cereals, dried milk, sugar, tea, coffee, flour and essential tins. We have found it generally better and to be a more efficient use of locker space to stow stores, including tins and other materials, in strong plastic bags rather than in cartons (see the reference to cockroaches below).

If you really have to take beef, lamb or pork etc. with you but have no freezer, it is possible to cook the meat and put it into bottles then cover it well with melted lard. Close the bottles tightly. This will keep for some time but store the bottles in a cool place and check now and then to make sure the lard is still sweet.

Try to avoid glass containers whenever possible but make sure the plastic (or other material) ones you use are really air/water tight (and so also virtually insect proof — though they will not stop resident weevils breeding in flour and pasta so don't keep such items for very long if bought abroad — those bought in affluent countries are usually fairly free).

It is now possible to buy two items which are a positive godsend when preserving soft fruit and vegetables on board. The first are packets of green "Everfresh" bags. These are Japanese in origin and will help keep vegetables and fruit in the fridge for a much longer period than otherwise. They will also preserve them out of the fridge but for a shorter period. Check every so often to make sure they are not going off. Also, if you see it, buy a new type of paper towel which is of a very thin sponge-like texture. It is advertised as being re-usable and indeed we use pads of the used paper to clean windows etc. (Wash, dry and re-use till worn out.) The variety we found is called "Home Cel".

You first wrap your fruit and vegetables separately in the "Home Cel" before you put them in the "Everfresh" bags. We have kept tomatoes, carrots, lettuce (specially the 'Iceberg' variety), spring onions, leeks, cauliflower and so on in this way in the fridge for several weeks. If you cannot find the sponge-paper then use ordinary kitchen towelling paper which also helps to keep the fruit and vegetables dry in the bags.   Incidentally, these bags also help to keep bread fresh for a little longer — check for mildew after a day or two.

We set great store by our pump-action vacuum flask (see Appendix 1). Buy the largest you can find (2 litres, almost 4 pints, is probably the biggest available). Ours proves invaluable, particularly on passage at night. We slip down to the galley while on watch and quickly pump out a cup of hot water to which we add instant soup, tea, coffee, Bovril or whatever we feel like. Avoiding the necessity to open the flask helps retain the heat for considerably longer than with a normal vacuum flask. However, if you cannot find a pump-action flask do take an ordinary one, if only to use at night. The large size is also useful for keeping ice for use with drinks.

On our ship, the Catering Officer has also to provide such items as pens, paper, pencils, envelopes, rubber bands, erasers, highlight pens and so on, so don't leave them off your list!

BELOW AND RIGHT *Our shopping trolley carries a vast amount, and can be hitched to the bicycle like a trailer.*

Shopping abroad

Shopping in the local markets can be quite an experience but great fun. Some of them are fabulous in the wealth of produce available and you should make an early opportunity to explore them. Try to find (probably before you leave home) some of the pocket travellers' guides for the countries you intend to visit. These not only give you some simple vocabulary (always good for a laugh!) but often also some good advice on local foods and specialities. Don't be afraid of asking the locals what is this or that — you will probably find they will fall over themselves trying to explain and to help you.

Try new foods — you will be surprised how good a ghastly-looking item tastes (or how truly dreadful some other rather odd thing really is!) Some local fruits and vegetables are delicious. For example Spain provides a fruit which we think is a peach-cross, called 'paraguayas'; in Turkey there are endless varieties of wild herbs and salad vegetables, some of them really delicious, and the Turks are always delighted to explain how to use them.

Have a good-sized folding shopping trolley — there is no need to carry when you can pull. You can often buy a locally made trolley in the market. Our bicycle-trailer combination has served us for years, and we highly recommend it.

Catering in hot climes

For everyday requirements it is best to buy in countries as you go. It is also fun to collect recipes from the countries you visit; people are only too happy to give details of local specialities, even in restaurants. Ask what foods are if you don't recognise them. Other yachties will provide information on what (and where) to buy in each port.

Regrettably, green salads are often very poor (or unavailable) in hot countries in summer, but sometimes you simply don't recognise local variants on temperate items such as radish. Wash all salads, fruit etc in a weak solution of potassium permanganate or in a baby-bottle sterilising solution such as "Milton 2" to be safe.

It is a good idea to keep one good basic recipe book on board for reference. You will also find interesting "local" recipe books in some countries which are often worth buying or borrowing. If you can get it, *Mediterranean Sea Food* by Davidson is very useful; although it says "Mediterranean" it is valid in most warm waters. This book is useful not only for identifying your own catch but also for recognising (and learning the local word for) a fish on display which is unfamiliar to you. It also gives a host of local recipes for fish from specific countries which is most useful.

Remember, if you are planning a long sea voyage you must store up — each yachtie has his/her own ideas of what to get and how to store it and is always willing to pass on 'wrinkles'. Listen well but do not follow advice blindly; make up your own mind.

It is easier to store foods in several smaller boxes or bags rather than in one large one which takes up more and more room as time goes on. Tins should be labelled clearly with permanent ink unless you are sure your bilge/locker is completely dry. Most importantly, keep a list of all stores and where they are stowed. Use it and cross off items as used. This truly is vital. If you don't, and unless you have a phenomenal memory, you will find yourself having to go through lockers again and again to remind yourself what you have left. Be very strict with yourself as to what you take. Don't go overboard for items you *think* you will use. It's best to be sure first. You can always stock up either when you reach a large cosmopolitan port, or on a visit home.

Furnishings and linen

Seat coverings and backs should be spongeable or readily removable for cleaning. We find Dralon lasts quite well for the settees which do get a lot of wear. Ours began to look shabby before they wore out. We now have a glazed cotton but are finding it rather susceptible to creasing, even though it is buttoned. Talking of buttons, try to make certain that covered buttons are not metal-based (unless you can get brass ones these days) for they rust if they get damp — which they will. Our wheelhouse covers are made of a plastic-backed folkweave type material which has lasted well except where it gets localised heavy use.

You will want some mattresses for the sunbathers on deck. We have some made of thin (about 1.5 in, or 8 cm) foam rubber, covered with colourful cotton, which dry quickly after use and are easily rinsed off when necessary. We have a rule that they must be covered by a towel if the would-be recumbent is coated with suntan oil! For bed coverings we use fitted bottom sheets on those berths which can remain permanently made-up, otherwise ordinary sheets. For top covering we move from a loose sheet to a sheet plus sleeping bag laid over, then to duvets (if necessary with a blanket on top) as the weather cools down. Muffin, the ship's cat, is an early indicator of when to increase the covers! She moves from her own basket to lying on the top of the duvet at the foot of our bed, thence (if allowed) to under it as winter approaches!

Laundry

This is probably the worst chore on board. Don't let the wash get too large. When practical, a little done reasonably often is preferable unless you know of a laundry or launderette although, even in faraway places, these can be very expensive. We tend to dump about two day's cast-offs into a bucket of soapy water for an overnight soak before finishing the job the next day since this keeps the volume down.

If you are on a long voyage and away from fresh water supplies for any length of time, soak the clothes in salt water and detergent then rinse them in fresh water (which can be re-used after to wash down windows or varnish). June

BELOW *Laundry day: a typical scene on the quay. The "butter churn" device that you may be able to identify is a sort of hand-cranked washing machine.*

will not rinse out in salt water as both she and Bill find they are apt to get salt sores, but of course if water is at a premium you may also do this. You should also try to collect water from heavy rainstorms (even a little helps). It often runs off sails in a good steady stream by the gooseneck.

The new high-density washing powders are ideal to carry with you as they are so concentrated and take up so little space.If you have space to stow one, a mini washing machine (e.g. ITT Mini-Wash) is an excellent investment even if you can only use it when A.C. power and water are both available, usually in a marina. However, if at all possible to stow, this Chief Steward sets even more value on the luxury of a small spin drier (eg. Siemens, Ariston etc). It speeds up the drying process so much, especially in inclement weather or when the skipper is itching to get to sea, and it avoids drips at any time.

Ironing is a bit of a luxury and when cruising is not always possible. We do the "important" things when in port and forget the rest.

Sewing repairs

There are always plenty of these so try to stow a small sewing machine on board. This will cope with most jobs apart from heavy sail or awning materials. Hand operated machines are more flexible than electric ones.

Garbage

Never throw plastic in any shape or form over the side! We have a rule that only three items are allowed overboard and those only in deep water when we are well away from land. These are bottles, filled with sea water so they will sink at once; any empty tins or drink cans, suitably punched full of holes to facilitate rapid sinking; and any peelings from fresh fruit or vegetables, or left-over food which will quickly decompose. Everything else is put into plastic bags which when full are firmly tied at the top (to keep out flies and other nasties) and stored in a safe, out-of-the-way place until we reach a harbour (we tuck them up near the bows). Why hasn't someone produced (invented is too strong a term) a simple garbage compactor for use on board yachts which would compress it into neat blocks to fit into purpose-made plastic bags which could (by the same machine) be evacuated of air and sealed?. The technology is simple; the cost could be reasonable and the benefits immeasurable.

Medical

The Chief Steward is usually the ship's doctor too unless the Skipper is suitably trained. It's best to make up your own medical kit, including all the usual bandages, dressings, a couple of slings, "butterfly plasters" (to hold edges of wounds together), disinfectants, ointments, commonly needed medicines including headache and migraine treatments, doses for upset stomachs, strain and sprain lotions and balms and the strongest safe relaxants/sedatives your doctor will prescribe. See Appendix 7 for a list of basic medical supplies.

A tooth problem is also to be feared when you are away from a dentist. It is now possible to buy D.I.Y. dental kits for emergency fillings; ask your dentist for advice. (We once tried "Polyfilla" but even after the patient had kept his mouth open for half-an-hour, it still had not set!)

Heat exhaustion can catch up occasionally; ordinary salt is no longer fashionable but there are various brands of oral re-hydration salts available. The symptoms are tiredness and general malaise.

Don't forget sea-sickness remedies — we swear by Stugeron — or use the "Seaband" wrist pressure-pads which also seem to work well.

Most important, don't forget burn treatment. For this we cannot praise too much the Nelson's homeopathic burn ointment obtainable from health shops and many pharmacies. Applied without delay, this ointment really does have amazingly effective results, not only for stove burns or similar but for nasty sunburned areas as well. Indeed, we have found that several homeopathic remedies thoroughly earn their inclusion in the medical kit, particularly Arnica (both ointment and tablets) for bruises.

We recommend you include some disposable hypodermic syringes/needles in your kit — not necessarily with a view to using them yourself but as an anti-AIDS safety precaution in case an injection is needed in a "suspect" place.

If your G.P. will agree to advise, you might show him the details of your proposed kit for his expert comment. Ask his advice about 'heavy' medication (e.g. antibiotics and pain killers). Make sure he understands that you may be far from medical aid and unable to reach it for several days.

In this connection, if you have a MF/HF radio, or can arrange a relay through your VHF or "ham" set, you can obtain medical advice by radio if you have a serious accident or other serious medical condition with which to deal. On MF or HF, call "PAN PAN PAN" on one of the emergency frequencies — you will probably use 2182 KHz unless you are a long way from a shore radio station or shipping route. You should call similarly on VHF Channel 16. You will be put in touch with medical advice and assistance will be directed to you if practical. If you are a radio "ham" you should be able to obtain similar assistance on your next schedule or, if you can trace two stations talking, you may be able to break in and get your message across.

Flies, bugs and creepy-crawlies

Mosquitoes and biting flies seem to be the worst nuisances. Australians will have the benefit of the marvellous "Aeroguard Personal Insect Repellant" if they have personal mozzies! Unfortunately, this is not readily available elsewhere and the rest of us have to do the best we can. There are sprays and lotions one can use: everyone has their own view on which is most effective. When sitting on deck in the evening, an oriental-type "mosquito coil" can help keep 'em away. These are also effective in sleeping cabins but ensure they are safely covered with a wire mesh in case anything falls on them (eg. bed-clothes) which could cause a fire. In some places it is possible to buy proper containers for holding burning coils, but these are not often seen. A simple alternative is to stand the coil holder on a plate and cover it with a metal kitchen sieve (first removing the handle if you wish).

It is possible to buy 12v "blue lights" which attract and kill flying insects. You can also get 12v versions of the electric devices which heat disposable pads impregnated with an insect repellant such as "Raid" (try camping or caravan accessory shops). If you draw a blank there it is possible to modify the 220v type by replacing the heating pad in the 220v unit with two ceramic resistors of about 15 to 18 ohms, each about 6 mm wide and deep and 38-44 mm long. The resistors should be wired in series. Modified in this way these devices use very little current (about 0.4 amps) but you may have to use your ingenuity to get the resistors to stick where they will heat the impregnated pad. Do not use a "super-glue" — i.e. one of the instant cyanoacrylate types — as these can give off cyanide gas when heated. Packets of the impregnated pads are fairly widely obtainable.

Other particular nasties are cockroaches: once you have these pests on board they can take some time to eradicate, often reappearing long after you think you have caught the lot.

Cardboard cartons often contain 'roach eggs so don't keep them on board unless you first thoroughly clean out and spray them. If you do get an infestation (they may fly on board or come off the quay) use roach hives and/or make little balls of boric acid mixed with condensed milk as soft as possible to allow them to hold their shape when rolled in the palm of your hand. Lay these in corners and cupboards where the insects are known to be. Alternatively you can mix the boric acid with sugar and sprinkle it into a flat plastic box or tray and put it into cupboards well away from food or pets. Wash your hands well after touching the boric acid.

Lastly, beware of getting a rat on board. If you suspect you may get one in a particular port, try not to lie alongside. If you are lying bow- or stern-to, or with ropes ashore, it is easy to make effective rat guards from large plastic funnels. Carry rat poison (very carefully stowed away in securely sealed container) and a good-sized box trap. Use both immediately the presence of a rodent is suspected: rodents can do immense damage to electric cable insulation (among other things) in double quick time. We collected a rat in Port Taufiq but managed to divert him with cubes of melon until we caught him. R.I.P! Even so, he devoured most of our supply of instant soup!

TOP *Large plastic funnels on the mooring lines make effective rat guards.*

RIGHT *A cat ladder will enable your cat to rescue itself if it falls into the water, provided you can teach the animal how to use it....*

Pets

This is a very personal matter but we have found that a cat is by far the most popular pet on board ship. Give it a place of its own, a litter tray, clean water, some grass (which can be bought in boxes ready to grow) and food at regular intervals and it will be quite happy. It also like a scratching board; if it insists on using the furniture (or your ropes) try rubbing some dry cat mint into the scratching board now and then — this works wonders.

Cats can (and do) fall overboard but are surprisingly good at getting themselves out when alongside a reasonable pontoon/quay. However, it is easy to dangle a 'cat ladder' over the side. This is a long piece of heavy netting, stretched at intervals with wooden dowels or battens. If possible (that is without getting yourself scratched to bits in the process) try to teach your cat how to use this. Some people toss the animal overboard from a dinghy near the ladder and allow it to swim for it, with a little encouragement if necessary. This is a drastic (but effective) solution. We were soft and held ours up to the ladder (getting thoroughly scratched in the process) and we doubt if it taught her what the ladder was for!

Dogs are not so easy. They need to be exercised (cats tear along the deck, the boom, up the forestay and all over the boat — the awnings make marvellous private trampolines!) Dogs won't use boxes, added to which they take up a great deal of room; but people do carry them and happily so.

Other pets (such as birds or small mammals) are relatively easy.

Do remember that if you leave your boat for a period the pet(s) will have to be left safely with either a kind neighbour or in good kennels — which is not always easy. Most importantly though, carrying a pet will preclude you from visiting any country with strict quarantine laws. These currently include the United Kingdom, Ireland, Malta and Australia. Cyprus does not mind as long as your animal remains in the marina; Gibraltar is happy as long as your pet has all the proper vaccinations and injections it should have under international law. The UK and Ireland (and the Channel Islands) currently have a quarantine limit of six months, Australia of one year and Malta has been known to insist the animal is put down at once (they shoot them). Other countries may have quarantine regulations of which we are unaware but all pets should, as a matter of basic common sense, have valid and properly documented inoculations.

Ask your veterinary surgeon to give you some worm tablets before you leave (and any other medication he thinks could be useful in an emergency). We carry a carefully stowed bottle of chloroform just in case there is need to put an end to suffering.

Deck life

Much of your time will be spent on deck, particularly if you have adequate awnings. For our part, breakfast is usually taken below before we sail, but lunch and dinner are served on deck if the weather is good. Barbecues are often popular. You can have one on the beach — often with other yachties

BELOW *Muffin, our ship's cat, in her sleeping quarters. Cats are by far the most popular shipboard pets.*

sharing an anchorage — but please be very aware of the fire risk and don't light fires in prohibited areas. On board, use one of the stainless steel barbecues which rig to hang over the water. (Stop cooking before the meat is black — there is a North Country saying "when the meat it brown it's doon, when it's black it's boogered"!)

It is fun to get together with other sea-cooks and plan a party, each bringing one dish plus several copies of their recipe. In Larnaca, during the winter, a barbecue was organised every second week, each boat bringing their own meat/fish and a dish for the 'communal' table. People brought interesting salads, cakes and starters, and one American lady brought a pudding each time (these were so popular that there was always a queue waiting for her arrival). Arising from the popularity of these various dishes, two contributors collected recipes from as many live-aboards as they could and made them into a most attractive book which was sold for a local charity; when we last heard it was coming up for its third printing.

Winter lay-by's are usually lots of fun. One year in Turkey all the marina live-aboards banded together and had a good time raising funds which, in the spring, they used to give a "Marina Day" for the boys from a local orphanage. We enjoyed getting together to organise it, we enjoyed the functions we laid on to raise money and we immensely enjoyed the day itself. An unexpected spin-off from this was that the local Turkish community became even more friendly and cooperative. The winter lay-by is certainly a big part of the cruising life!

Generally speaking we find (with a few exceptions) that when we eat ashore the small eating places patronised by the locals prove to be much better value than the more affluent tourist ones. Naturally we occasionally splash out on a recommended and really good, expensive establishment — there is usually one to be found for that special occasion. Of course you have to try the local delicacies. Think of real Turkish Delight and genuine Indian or Malay curries!

We swim as and when convenient (and depending on water temperature) but often twice a day. Nothing is nicer than a moonlight swim before the bed-time nightcap. The solar-heated shower bags mentioned earlier are excellent and remarkably economical with the water: but do remember the warning about them getting too hot. Ensure the crew don't over-do the sun; guests in particular may not realise the perils and the full-time crew should remember the hazard of skin cancers and other nasties. Take good sunglasses with you — the brightness from sun and water can be extreme.

Guests and entertaining

It's fun to have family and friends visit for a week or two. However, guard against the seductive trap of allowing guests to distort your cruising plans too severely. By all means make it as easy as possible for them to join you and at the end to get back to their 'plane or whatever, but do arrange beforehand that the visitors will travel under their own steam and not expect the ship to take the strain.

Don't make arrangements early on to meet on a certain date at a specific point. Try to leave these arrangements as late as possible, phoning to settle last minute details. Remember there is always the risk that either the yacht will be early and have to wait around for the guests or, perhaps worse, will be late and the guests will have to check into an hotel until it arrives — they should be warned about this.

Make certain that the guests do understand the limitations of the yacht (the undesirability of hard suitcases etc.) and that they are sensibly economical with the amount of clothing they bring. Remember to ask them to bring soft-soled shoes. Non-yachties will need discreet guidance on such points.

Guests on board, particularly non-sailors or first-time visitors, should also be told the important aspects of living on board such as conservation of water, safety aspects (particularly concerning gas in case they offer to put on the kettle) and the position of fire extinguishers, lifebelts etc. This can be in the form of a light-hearted sheet: see ours in Appendix 3.

Finally, the most sensitive point of all — cost. You may find that you have guests for a total of eight to ten weeks in the season. This can put a real strain on your finances which is frequently not realised by your friends. We have found that if a "kitty" system is diplomatically suggested when the possibility of a visit is first mooted, everyone is very much happier. However, be sure not to make the existence of a kitty obvious to local authorities — some may choose to consider this as evidence that you are chartering, thus laying you open to a host of problems. If your finances can take the strain, that's fine.

8

THE PAPERWORK
Oiling the wheels

- Ship's stamp
- Crew lists
- Ship's details and register
- Stores and equipment lists
- Copies of important documents
- Maintenance and spares registers
- Visitors' book
- Library

Ship's stamp

You must have a ship's stamp prepared: the kind of rubber stamp used with an ink pad. Make it as simple or as imposing as you like. Its use will be requested by many officials to "validate" the innumerable forms you will be asked to complete and/or sign — without the stamp the document might not be considered "legal"! This isn't in the "fun to have" category: believe us, it's an essential in many places and certainly eases the way in others. The Captain's signature over the ship's stamp is unarguably official.

Crew lists

You will need a considerable number of copies of your crew list: many countries must be sinking into the sea with the number on file! We recommend that you head the list with brief details of the ship, then list permanent crew leaving space for visitors to be added. Finish with a summary of the numbers on board and leave space for the Captain's signature over the ship's official stamp. A layout might be as opposite.

Have this typed and photocopied. We recommend that you start with at least 30 copies — to use five in one port is not unusual and we mean port, not country! If friends join you, initially add their details to a couple of copies in case you are asked but put them down as crew, not as passengers. If you put them under the "passenger" category, you risk being held to be chartering with all the potentially horrific consequences thereof (see Chapter 2).

Ship's details and register

It can make life a lot easier if you have an extract of the ship's register and other details to take with you when you report to customs etc. You will very likely find that no two ports in any single country ask for the same information: in some countries once you have "entered in" you are finished until you leave; in others you have to "enter" and "clear" at each port although not necessarily with the same amount of detail. Thus you never know which details the authorities will choose to record.

They only rarely ask to see the actual official papers but they will want you to fill in their form requiring the Official Number, port of registry, date built, where built, G.R.T. and N.R.T, L.O.A., beam, depth (yes! depth — invent it if you have to), draft, type and serial number of engine(s), horsepower or capacity of engine(s), and anything else which the designer of the form thought would be "useful"! This skipper invariably forgets one or other of the numbers so takes a briefing paper and the ship's stamp with him.

Stores and equipment lists

Some Customs Authorities require fairly detailed inventories of the ship's equipment — both fixed and movable. This is largely to make it difficult for gear imported on a "duty free" concession (which includes the ship) to be sold or otherwise disposed of in their country. This is understandable, although the extent of detail they require can be tiresome to say the least. However, there is some positive spin-off from the preparation of this inventory: it is illuminating to set down just how much you do have on board and it can be a great help when dealing with your underwriters. A copy of our list — specially annotated with the dates of acquisition and individual values — is lodged with our brokers.

For use of the Authorities, the list gives the serial numbers of equipment when they exist but not the value, for obvious reasons. In the event of theft, it is helpful to be able to give serial numbers to the police. We have run off

Yacht "NEVERWOZ"

Utopian Flag	**Port of Registry: Atlantis.**	**Official No.1234560**
G.R.T. 27.65	N.R.T. 19.2t	Auxiliary Schooner

CREW LIST

Names	Nationality	Place & Date of Birth	Passport No & Issued at
Bloggs, John	Utopian	Wagga 30 Feb. '01	4017346D Wagga
Bloggs, Anne	Utopian	Stump 32 Dec. '06	4122793D Wagga

(add friends' names here as CREW when on board)

PASSENGER LIST

NIL

Total Crew: Two (2) **Signed** ....

Total Passengers: Nil (0) (Master)

Date ....

ABOVE *A suggested layout for a crew list. Note that you never carry passengers.*

two or three copies for handing over: with a little persuasion the Authorities will attach your copy to their documentation (provided each page is signed over the ship's stamp!) instead of making you copy it in full on to their own forms.

It is difficult to advise how much detail you should include but you should definitely list all major gear plus firearms, scuba gear, portable radios, TV/VCR, computer, bicycles, motor scooters, cameras, binoculars (even though some of these are not strictly ship's gear) and cover other items under a generic description such as "other miscellaneous ship and personal equipment E. & O.E." We have never had any difficulty as a result of doing this although we certainly only give the list if it is clearly an official requirement. Yes, it is a chore, but once it is done it is no hardship to supply copies and, after all, you are asking to be a guest in their country...

Copies of important documents

We have found it to be very useful to have photocopies of all important documents including the Ship's Certificate of Registration, Bill of Sale, insurance policies (ship and personal), radio licence(s), V.A.T. or other tax receipts, customs' clearance from home country (if issued), passports, driving licences, a list of credit/cash cards and anything else of which you may wish to have a record. One copy of these can be kept in the "panic bag" (Chapter 5), another left with your family or bank at home and a third copy put away safely on board.

We had the misfortune to be robbed in Seville of a bag which contained our passports and driving licences. (As an aside, beware of the thieves who operate on motor cycles: the pillion rider leaps off, grabs your bag and leaps on again. The thieves carry knives which they are not reluctant to use — on the straps of the bag or on you if you are quick enough to resist. But back to our example...)

We had photocopies of all our documents on board. The copies of our passports supported by a copy of the police report of the theft enabled us to draw cash from banks and to leave Spain and enter Gibraltar en route back to Spain. Our photocopy driving licences were acceptable when we hired cars and it was only when we had to re-enter the UK that we encountered bureaucracy and (until we refused to accept it) ill-mannered behaviour on the part of the petty official at the British Consulate. Photocopying

also means that you have all the required serial numbers, dates and so on needed to replace the papers.

Maintenance and spares registers

We have found it very useful to have a register of work carried out on board: engine oil changes, filter changes, injector servicing, equipment repairs or installation, rigging or sail repair/overhaul, cutlass bearing change, accommodation refurbishment and so on. Ours is kept under appropriate headings such as "Main Engine", "Generator", "Electronic Equipment", "Domestic Equipment" and "Hull". Each entry is dated (with engine hours run if appropriate) and approximate costs shown. Not only is this an invaluable aid when planning maintenance but it also allows you to keep a check on reliability. We have even been able to claim on suppliers for replacement of a defective part based on the record.

We also keep a register of spares carried, where they are stowed, the cost price and the supplier's name and address where relevant. This, too, is well worth the minor work involved in keeping it up for, with the need to hold a considerable stock of spares, an index to stock levels and stowages saves many a fruitless hunt.

When we bought our present boat *Ros Arcan,* there was a goodly quantity of spares of one sort or another so we set-to making lists as we organised ourselves on board. We had not tackled one last locker up forward beyond a cursory look and anyway Bill knew there was nothing of importance in it: just bits and pieces, some rolled veneer and a package of veneer, and so on, nothing that needed early attention...

Half-way through our second season a cylinder head gasket blew and we limped into Malta. We had no spare gaskets but Manoel Island Yacht Yard knew who to contact in the UK for spares. Then Murphy came into the picture as he does in such circumstances: the spares supplier had just closed for his annual two-week holiday! We enjoyed our stay in Malta — we had intended to go there anyway but not necessarily in midsummer — and eventually got the job done.

Later that same year, that final locker was cleared and its contents listed and stowed as appropriate. There was one red face on board though: the parcel of veneers turned out to be a cylinder head overhaul kit complete with TWO sets of gaskets!

One further useful attribute of a spares register is that it forms the basis for your shopping list when you are in a port where the shopping is good.

Visitors' book

A visitors' book is a source of many happy memories. We recommend you buy a nice fat book with plain pages, about international A4 size. It soon grows into a veritable story book. When time allows, your non-resident guests can take it away for a day or two and fill a page with their details, photographs or drawings, doggerel verse or worse and so on. Some of the books on these lines that we have seen are veritable gems in their way: we, alas, failed to start one of our own until it was too late.

Library

Take a good selection of books with you even if you have already read them. You will find that most cruising yachts are very anxious to swap and "Have you any books to change?" is often the first question after the greeting.

9 THE NAVIGATOR'S LOT
Skills and equipment

- Your level of competence
- Chart table and equipment
- "Essential" electronics
- Charts and pilots
- Navigation lights
- Communications and weather

Your level of competence

Leaving aside the longer passages en route to your chosen cruising ground, you will very likely be out of sight of land for several hours or longer while coast or island hopping: either because the headlands or islands are 30 miles or more apart, because you have to make one of your occasional overnight passages or even because visibility is poor. Don't expect totally clear horizons in the warmer seas: it may be a lovely day with a calm sea, pleasant breeze and bright sunshine; then you suddenly realise that horizontal visibility is only 2 or 3 miles — how else could that large ship have suddenly appeared? So although much, maybe most, of your navigation is coastal pilotage you will at least have to work up a D.R. to an acceptable standard. It is only too easy to become rusty in these matters and, as recommended in Chapter 2, it may be worth taking a refresher course to brush up your navigation.

Chart table and equipment

These are just some of our experiences — no lesson is intended.We believe it is necessary to have a chart table which is sufficiently large to take a British Admiralty chart on half-fold horizontally. Believe it or not, our previous fine and much-loved 38-foot ketch didn't have a chart table at all when we bought her. We built one into her half-wheelhouse opposite the steering position so it became possible for the navigator to see all around from his station and the watch-keeper to run his plot without burying himself below. This really is an excellent arrangement, particularly for coastal pilotage when you may need to make frequent reference to the chart and pilot book.

ABOVE *The chart table aboard* Ros Arcan, *showing the shock cord restraints to hold the charts.*

You may be able to fit a light, if necessary removable, chart table in your steering area. Many yachts have a table attached to the steering wheel column and this may suffice or be slightly modified to fit the bill. It is well worth the effort even if it is a second and makeshift chart table.

As to instruments, you will need all the usual ones but since you will probably be laying off quite a few bearings, you may find a station pointer useful. You will also need a good, easy-to-use hand-bearing compass. (If you haven't already got one, bear in mind our earlier comment in the paragraph on RDF in Chapter 6). The hand-bearing compass should have its stowage position by the watch-keeper, as should a good pair of binoculars — neither are much use at a chart table down below.

One lesson we have learned is the desirability of being able to keep your charts, parallel ruler, plotting triangle and whatever securely on the chart table when the ship is bouncing all over the seas. Shock cord is a great help with this problem and it can easily be rigged or removed as necessary. Pencils, dividers, compasses, erasers (we have learned not to refer to 'rubbers' to avoid misleading our American friends!) can be kept securely in one of the plastic holders sold in chandlers all over the world or in one of your own design and making.

"Essential" electronics

We have discussed many aspects of electronic aids in Chapter 6 and will try to avoid repetition here. Clearly you should have an echo sounder, the first electronic instrument of all — anything else is a bonus!

For coastal use, there must be little to beat radar with its ability to help you fix your position with considerable accuracy. Bear in mind that radar can give you a single-point fix using the bearing and range markers in conjunction with each other. All-in-all, it is a great boon and is generally very reliable too. Keep in mind our comments on misleading visibility — we use our radar on more passages than we don't.

The GPS satellite system is a coastal (and deep-sea) navigation system of considerable note but forget the Transit satellite system for coastal work. Loran C (or Decca if you are in an operational area) gives virtually continuous position fixing and both are discussed in Chapter 6.

Whatever electronic aid you are using, make a practice of noting your position every hour (when you read your log) while also keeping a D.R. or position line plot. This "belt and braces system" has proved its worth to us on a number of occasions when it became obvious that one of the "magic boxes" had developed a glitch. One finds that Loran stations, for example, can be closed down temporarily for maintenance purposes: this is usually just when you are looking for a position!

Charts and pilots

Here we have an unavoidable and quite considerable expense. With British Admiralty charts having breached the £10 barrier, your investment in charts will equal the cost of Loran C receiver or even a GPS set but there is little you can do about it. Of all the possible economies that can be made, we feel that to skimp on charts is akin to being a foolish virgin (without the subsequent pleasure!)

There is no need to carry the largest-scale ones for an area unless it is a particularly hazardous or difficult piece of water. This is particularly so if you are able to buy a good yachting pilot of which there are now an increasing number; these are also very expensive but, believe me, they are not a profitable occupation for their authors. Check

your chosen pilot for detail and if the plans of ports, narrow channels, anchorages etc. look pretty detailed then it should not be necessary to buy a large-scale chart. However, prudence dictates that when piloting using the sketches or photographs in a yachting pilot (or guide as some publishers prefer to call them) you should take particular care. Most yachting pilot authors are very careful about the information they give and many give a deal more than the official charts and pilots, but they can and do make mistakes or miss something. If you run ashore in consequence, be it on your own head.

Please play your own part in maintaining the accuracy of the information contained in the various yachting pilots (and in the "official" ones too). The private authors and the British Hydrographer to the Navy are equally grateful for any reports that correct or amplify information in their publications. If you find an error or new development in your travels but merely grumble that it "should have been reported" and do no more, you deserve all you get.

It is possible that there are charts produced by the Administration of the area in which you are cruising: these may well be considerably cheaper than the British, French, U.S. or Australian equivalents. On occasion they may be more detailed or accurate and they are certainly worth looking at. However, more often than not, you get what you pay for and, as a generalisation, the charts and publications from the leading maritime countries are far and away the best value for money.

When you approach or reach your cruising area, you will be able to buy charts from other yachties and this source should not be overlooked. They will most probably be well out-dated and you may be the sixth owner! However, dependent on the area, and provided that you have a decent pilot and, if possible, an up-to-date lights list, they may well be adequate.

You will often be offered photocopies too. Technically these are illegal but there are plenty of them about and considering the cost of the real thing it is not surprising. They are not, of course, likely to be remotely up-to-date or even a recent edition but sometimes they are all that is available. Bear in mind, however, that if you run ashore and damage or lose your ship, your underwriters are at liberty to declare the insurance null and void as you can be held not to have taken the care required of you!

Charts are so valuable nowadays that it's worth trying to keep them up-to-date. We go to considerable trouble to obtain the British Admiralty's weekly *Notices to Mariners* issued gratis by the British Hydrographer and to correct our chart stock (which well exceeded 100 at last count, new value in excess of £1100!). Applying the corrections can only be done as and when the *Notices* are received, perhaps three times a year at best. It is a chore but in our view it is very worthwhile.

Communications and weather

We recommend that you make full use of Navtex if you have it and it is operational in your area. It should give you weather and important navigational information such as failed lights, floating debris of danger to navigation, off-limits areas and so on. Such information is also often broadcast by coast radio stations at scheduled times over VHF and MF/HF. You can obtain details of broadcasts from official publications and commercial nautical almanacs such as Reed's for Northern Europe to Gibraltar, the Mediterranean and the North American east Coast. Do not forget other national publications such as the French Votre Livre de Bord and so on.

The Amateur Maritime Mobile nets also disseminate weather and general information often to be found nowhere else: we have discussed this source in Chapter 6. If you do not have the means to obtain Weatherfax data, you can almost certainly get the benefit of another boat's pictures and interpretations by tuning into the Ham nets.

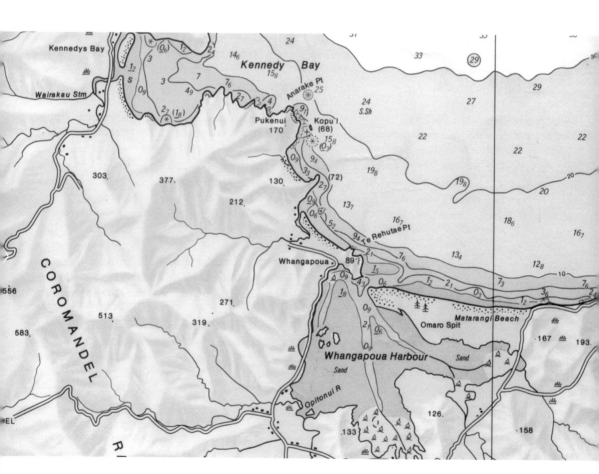

10 OFFICERS AND DECKIES
Handling the boat

- Navigation lights
- Siren (horn)
- Flags and bunting
- Rules of the Road
- Anchoring
- Manoeuvering under power and berthing
- Lying alongside and unberthing
- Ropes and lines
- Hardware
- Security

We are not setting out to write a manual of seamanship in these few pages, rather to give some comments/advice on matters you may not have experienced or contemplated before and which might be useful.

Navigation lights

We have already mentioned navigation lights but the subject stands amplification and some repetition. Don't use "toy" ones. The Collision Regulations prescribe the "luminous intensity" required for each light and these are not difficult to meet if only someone will convert them into a value we simpletons can understand! Fortunately, the principal suppliers have done this for us (e.g. Aquasignal).

Use lights correctly; this again presents no difficulty and is appreciated by other responsible mariners. One particularly irritating — and in fact dangerous — malpractice is the concurrent use of both a masthead tricolour and lower-mounted lights intended for use when not under sail. One set or the other, please, not both! Some Authorities have purges when they check that yachts carry all-round reds, whites and greens although we have never been queried. (It would be a good idea if those same authorities looked at their own fishermen!)

A powerful hand-held or deck-mounted searchlight (e.g. Aquasignal, Francis, Par Jabsco etc) will help when entering strange anchorages on a dark night — not everyone uses an anchor light. It is also useful for attracting the attention of a rogue ship not keeping proper look-out, or finding the source of a close unidentified 'blip' on the radar.

We strongly recommend the use of an anchor light, even if your anchorage does seem to be a deserted spot. If you are worried about power consumption, you can buy a light with an integral light-sensing switch which switches it on at dusk and off at dawn. Aquasignal recommend that one of their 10 watt bulbs meets the technical requirement: this would consume about 10 amps during an average night which is not too severe a price to pay. An all-round white masthead light is legitimate as an anchor light and is frequently used.

Siren (horn)

If a siren is not a fixed item, stow a good hand model. The ones that use disposable air cartridges are good and are now available with ozone-friendly gas. Carry spare cartridge(s); you might be surprised how often you need to use the thing to wake up someone (frequently a tripper boat) trying to ignore your presence.

Flags and bunting

Please wear a good-sized national ensign even if (oh horror!) you don't always hand it at sunset as you should. Also, it is only polite to fly at the starboard cross-tree (spreader) a reasonably-sized Maritime ensign of your host country. Unfortunately, some countries choose to be hyper-sensitive about their flags: in Rhodes — not renowned for its courtesies — we were summarily fined £30 for flying a very slightly frayed Greek ensign even though we had only arrived late the previous evening and had already bought a new one but had not had time to change it. (The plethora of Greek-flag ships — and the Town Hall, Bishop's Palace etc — with extremely ragged Greek flags were apparently exempt!) We stress maritime ensigns because some countries such as the UK and Malta have different national flags for different purposes.

It is sometimes possible to buy cotton "flag netting" which you sew to the edge of the "fly" of any flag that gets considerable use. This netting takes the wear of flapping in the wind thus saving the flag itself (and maybe a fine!) If you cannot buy something suitable, you can make up some of your own using either fishermen's net-making knots or (filet) crocheting. We were able to find coloured yarn to match both our red and blue ensigns: its presence is unnoticeable at more than a few feet away. For club burgees, national courtesy flags and so on, a fairly thin white yarn is suitable and, at masthead or spreader height, is also practically invisible.

If you can stretch to a complete set of code flags, try hard to dress ship on national or local special days — the practice is very much appreciated by your hosts. Even if you don't have a full set of flags, you will need code flag "Q" for arrival purposes.

We make a point of dipping our ensign to warships of our host nation met at sea: it is always well-received with a return dip followed by much hand-waving. We're sure you know how to do it, but in case you need a refresher, you wait until the warship is nearly abeam and certainly can see you, then dip your national ensign to half-staff or whatever. Next you will probably see a sailor on the warship running aft at great speed; the warship's ensign is dipped and held momentarily, then closed up again. Only then do you return your ensign to its "closed-up" position and go back to your gin.

A practice becoming increasingly common is for yachts carrying nationals other than those from the ship's provenance or host nation to wear their "foreign visitor's" ensign(s) at the port cross-tree. We haven't seen any official line on this but, to our mind, it is both a nice courtesy and a useful indication of who's who.

Rules of the Road

It goes without saying that you should be *au fait* with and obey the Collision Regulations. Alas, this does not mean that everyone else will be similarly guided but at least you will recognise who is doing what and be able to react appropriately. Others should also recognize what *you* are doing. The rules dealing with potential collisions are particularly relevant although, if your experience is like ours, might is too often construed as right. Ferries, in particular, seem to make their own rules so beware.

Here lie the bones of Mike O'Day
Who died preserving his right of way.

Seriously, the skipper should be comfortable with the Rules and the standing order to other crew must be "if in doubt, call me."

Anchoring

We have already made the point that properly-sized ground tackle is essential; err on the larger size if in doubt. We have also stressed the desirability of having a windlass and (if possible) self-stowing anchors and cable. Unfortunately, there are not many yachts whose chain locker will accept a large intake of chain without having someone to help it to flake down. You will probably find that there is a certain amount of chain that will self-stow, after which it becomes unruly. One hazard of going beyond this critical length is that the chain will build a pyramid. You then go to sea, the ship rolls and bounces a bit, the pyramid collapses and when you next try to let go you find the chain has jammed under itself — just when you need it most.

Now to deal with choosing where to let go and how to set your anchor. You will clearly choose to anchor under the lee of the land or in a bay if possible, but bear in mind that the wind will probably shift during the night: your experience of local conditions will guide you on this point. Also bear in mind the direction of the swell — some anchorages never seem to be free of it even though they are apparently well-sheltered.

Having decided that the other yacht has grabbed the best place, you must make do with second best. The chances are that the water will be sufficiently clear for you to see the bottom, in which case have the foredeck hand direct you to a sandy patch if there is one, clear of weed and rocks. If you are anchoring in a coral area, *please take every possible care not to drop Old Coldnose on to coral.* Indiscriminate anchoring over coral is causing untold damage in some areas of the world: there should be a spot where your anchor can dig in to good ground without breaking off coral heads.

It appears to be increasingly common practice to let go while still steaming ahead. This may well set the anchor firmly but can do your topsides no good at all and unless you have positioned yourself carefully, the anchor will have to break out and re-set when you drop back on the chain. We, and most other old salts, still stop the ship over the spot where we wish the anchor to lie, let go and then go astern (blow astern downwind if under sail) to lay out the chain before making sure the anchor is properly set by going hard astern until the chain is taut. In the warm (we hope) waters you are sailing, one of the first swimmers can check the anchor is dug in, or as is often the case with a CQR, is well set to dig in when the strain comes on to it.

So you've got your anchor set (whereupon 'Murphy' sees to it that the other yacht — the one in the best position — leaves!) but how much scope have you laid and how much should you have? The old rules of thumb are three times the depth at high water with chain, and five times with a chain/rope combination. This is fine in a good depth but inadequate in shallow water unless the holding ground is very good. The catenary effect is the important bit — it ensures the pull on the anchor is as near to horizontal as possible and it also acts as a "spring" to cushion the snatching if the vessel is sheering about. If the angle between the chain or chain/rope and the sea bed exceeds 10% where the chain joins the anchor, the holding power of the anchor is reduced to 60% or less of its potential maximum. There is a geometric formula which can be applied to this:

FOR CHAIN: 12 x sq.root of depth in metres at high water

FOR CHAIN/ROPE: 20 x sq.root of depth in metres at high water

For convenient reference, below left is a table based on these formulae, a copy of which you might like to keep handy.

There are various ways of marking your chain: we chose to do it in 5-fathom stages, but only because fathoms were in vogue when we first marked it. We suggest that, if you are marking your chain anew, you set the marks at 10-metre or 5-fathom intervals to your preference.

Our suggested system is to paint stripes on the chain in about 6-in (15-cm) lengths as follows according to whether you are working in metres or fathoms/feet:

20 m	10 fthms	one yellow stripe
30 m	15 fthms	two yellow stripes
40 m	20 fthms	one green stripe
50 m	25 fthms	two green stripes
60 m	30 fthms	one red stripe
70 m	35 fthms	two red stripes
80 m	40 fthms	one blue stripe

(and so on if you have that much scope)

This system is pretty easy to remember as it progresses in 10-metre or 5-fathom steps and the helmsman only has to tell the foredeck hand to let go "one green on deck" or "two yellows in the water" or whatever.

If anchorage space is confined, you can restrict the ship's swinging circle by putting down two anchors in a running moor. To us, this is a "running boor" to be avoided whenever possible as you inevitably seem to end up with your cables wrapped around each other.

Alternatively, you will find many popular anchorages where the custom is to anchor and then take a rope ashore to a convenient palm or olive tree, rock or, if necessary, to a buried kedge. In these circumstances, ensure

DEPTH AT HIGH WATER		ALL CHAIN		CHAIN AND ROPE	
metres	feet	metres	fthms	metres	fthms
4.5	15	25.5	14.0	42.5	23.0
6.0	20	29.5	16.5	50.0	27.5
7.5	25	33.0	18.5	55.0	30.0
9.0	30	36.0	20.0	60.0	33.0
10.5	35	39.0	21.5	65.0	35.5
12.0	40	41.5	23.0	69.0	38.0
13.5	45	44.0	24.5	73.5	40.0
15.0	50	46.5	26.0	77.5	42.5
16.5	55	49.0	27.0	81.0	44.4
18.0	60	51.0	28.3	84.5	46.0
19.5	65	53.0	29.5	88.5	48.5

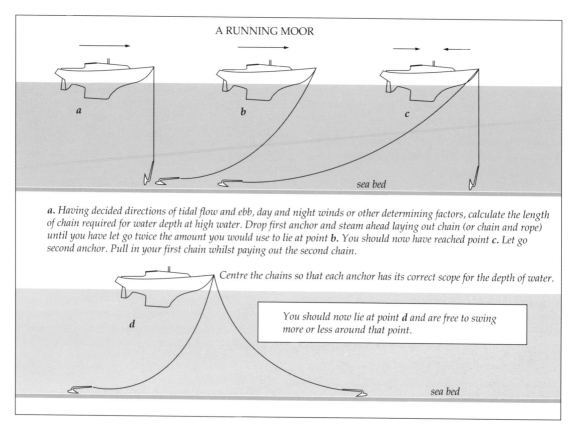

A RUNNING MOOR

a. *Having decided directions of tidal flow and ebb, day and night winds or other determining factors, calculate the length of chain required for water depth at high water. Drop first anchor and steam ahead laying out chain (or chain and rope) until you have let go twice the amount you would use to lie at point* **b.** *You should now have reached point* **c.** *Let go second anchor. Pull in your first chain whilst paying out the second chain.*

Centre the chains so that each anchor has its correct scope for the depth of water.

You should now lie at point **d** *and are free to swing more or less around that point.*

sea bed

your anchor has plenty of scope and is well set: you can bet a beam wind will blow up in the night putting considerable strain on gear and often causing the anchor to shift. We heartily dislike making up like this but it is occasionally unavoidable. (We have also commented on this problem in Chapter 4). When you have a line ashore, mark it at intervals as necessary with buoy(s) — fenders will do (and worn out rubber gloves are popular!) — as a precaution against someone trying to pass between you and the shore.

If the anchorage is busy or if the bottom is known to be foul, consider if you should rig a trip line to your anchor. We have very mixed feelings about these as the trip line can itself become snagged — particularly if there is a substantial rise and fall of tide. The use of an anchor buoy is probably better but use a reasonably strong line attached to the anchor's crown so you can trip it out of a snag if necessary. Be sure to mark the anchor buoy with an anchor and the ship's name otherwise someone will make up to it! The trip line should be as long as the approximate depth of

water at high tide plus a couple of metres maximum: any substantial surplus line should be coiled and tightly lashed to the buoy.

We now turn to how to free your anchor if it is caught under someone else's chain — either because they have laid theirs across yours or because one has dragged under the other. We once had no fewer than four chains across ours! In this connection, be careful when weighing that you don't steam over the ground while breaking out your "hook". This is a guaranteed way to pick up another chain. The same thing applies when letting-go. Put your anchor down cleanly with some (not too much) slack chain so that when you do go astern to set the anchor it will not drudge over the bottom.

To free your snagged anchor from under another chain, ask the other yacht to slack away his chain which will enable you to haul your anchor and his chain to the surface without disturbing the other ship's anchor. Having pulled the offending chain to the surface, pass a line under

BELOW *A common sight in crowded anchorages — the hook coming up with someone else's chain draped across it.*

RIGHT *The solution. Ask the other yacht to slacken off his chain, get a rope around it and secure the rope aboard at both ends. Then slacken off your own anchor to free the snag, haul the anchor aboard and finally release the rope to allow your neighbour's chain to sink back to the sea bed.*

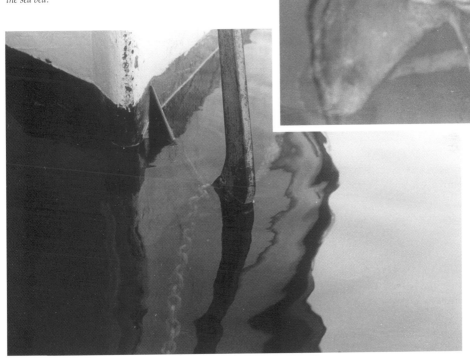

it and back on board, making the line fast at both ends. Then slack away on your anchor slowly until you can unhook it and get it on board. Only then should you let go one end of your line so allowing the other boat's chain to fall back to the bottom; he can then take up the slack. The same process applies to snags on moorings except that it will not be possible to slack off the offending chain and the weight to lift will be correspondingly greater. Of course, if one of you is a scuba diver the problems are halved...

Now let us deal with lying beam-on to a swell. It is amazing how it can penetrate and spoil an otherwise perfect spot. Invariably the wind seems to be across the swell (or becomes so in the evening) and the ship lies into the wind. If the wind is likely to remain steady you can adjust the direction of the ship's head by taking a line between the cable and the after-end of your ship, tightening it until she is pulled round to the required angle. This is effective only if the wind direction is constant: if the wind shifts so does the heading of your ship and the rolling begins all over again!

Another method is to lay a light kedge from the stern (or your normal kedge on a short scope) to hold the yacht's bow into the swell. The idea is that the kedge will drag if the wind gets up and allow the boat to swing to it,

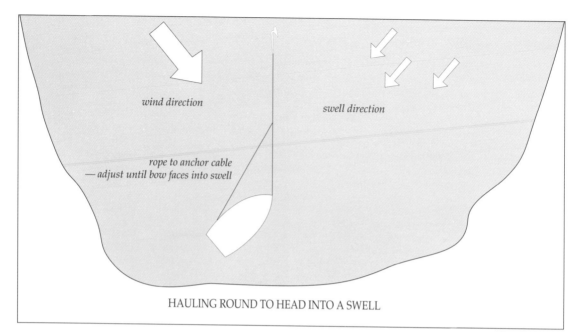

wind direction

swell direction

*rope to anchor cable
— adjust until bow faces into swell*

HAULING ROUND TO HEAD INTO A SWELL

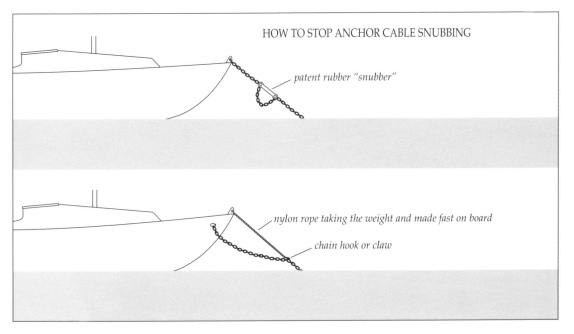

HOW TO STOP ANCHOR CABLE SNUBBING

patent rubber "snubber"

nylon rope taking the weight and made fast on board

chain hook or claw

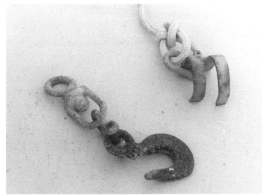

both avoiding unfair strains on the bower and warning you of the freshening weather.

The annoyance of chain cable snatching and growling in the hawse or on the stemhead roller can be avoided by fastening one (or if necessary two) heavy rubber snubbers between the chain just outboard of the boat and say four feet (a metre and a quarter) nearer to the sea. If this is arranged so that the chain hangs in a slight bight, any snubbing will be absorbed by the rubber but the chain is always there to take the full load if necessary. The rigging of this arrangement is facilitated by the use of a chain claw or hook. Alternatively, in a heavy surge use nylon rope instead of the rubber-snubber and bring its upper end on board to a strong cleat. This allows you to have a longer bight of chain knowing that the rope will carry away and the ship fall back onto the chain if things really get tough.

Chain hooks and claws are useful devices for holding the chain cable temporarily in most circumstances — for instance if for some reason (such as servicing the windlass or freeing a cable jam) you need to take the weight off the gypsy.

TOP LEFT *A chain hook and chain claw.*
LEFT *A chain claw taking the weight of the anchor cable to free the windlass for servicing.*

ABOVE *A pair of snatch blocks are essential equipment for all kinds of tasks. Here they are shown open (left) and closed.*
RIGHT *An inflatable cone shape for motor-sailing.*

When at anchor, you should have a black anchor ball shape in the forepart of the ship (the anchor light can be rigged on the same halyard but just above it). You can buy a collapsible plastic shape or make your own very easily out of plywood. Incidentally, while on the subject of "shapes", you should also have a black cone for use when you are motor-sailing. You can readily make a collapsible plywood one or buy a plastic or inflatable one.

BELOW *A collapsible anchor ball rigged and collapsed (right).*

Manoeuvring under power and berthing

You will inevitably have to handle your ship in very confined quarters: the constraints are likely to be floating ropes, moorings and anchor cables rather than other vessels, so you may not be able to hand your boat clear but will have to rely on cautious engine movements.

Practice manoeuvring in quiet conditions and learn how to exploit the propeller effect which swings your stern one way or the other according to the propeller's direction of rotation. You should aim at being able to turn your ship within a length and a half by using full ahead and full astern movements in short bursts. Remember that while technically there is a pivotal point about which your ship turns, it is primarily the stern that moves around the bow. Learn the effects of wind which can frustrate your efforts and always plan ahead whether you intend to turn to port or to starboard. Even the windage of a person standing upright on the foredeck can make life very difficult.

'Close-quarters' handling is a skill you can learn if you practise and study your ship's behaviour. It is very satisfying to put your vessel precisely and neatly where you want her while under the critical gaze of your fellow yachties. It's good even if no one is watching!

When berthing alongside it makes life much easier if you berth head-to-wind and get the head-rope ashore first. Getting the stern in is easy: if all is really going well that day a short burst astern will screw her in but if the propeller effect swings her off, or if the wind is blowing her stern off, gently steaming against the (secured) head-rope with the helm over as if to turn her bow off will have the

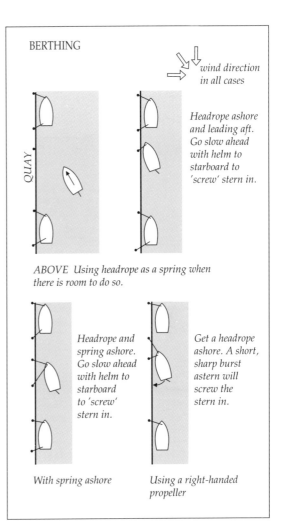

BERTHING

wind direction in all cases

QUAY

Headrope ashore and leading aft. Go slow ahead with helm to starboard to 'screw' stern in.

ABOVE Using headrope as a spring when there is room to do so.

Headrope and spring ashore. Go slow ahead with helm to starboard to 'screw' stern in.

Get a headrope ashore. A short, sharp burst astern will screw the stern in.

With spring ashore

Using a right-handed propeller

effect of bringing her stern in. Or, of course, it is better if you temporarily lead your head-rope aft or get a spring ashore but untutored shore-helpers don't always understand what you want them to do. These two latter options achieve the same purpose of letting you pull in your stern with the added benefit of preventing the yacht from moving forward. Whenever you use the springing technique, put fenders well forward as the bow will come hard against the quay.

It is customary in the Mediterranean (and in many other places) to moor end-on to the quay. The first question is, do you choose to berth bow-to or stern-to? Frankly, it is up to you: bow-to is sometimes easier — indeed, we have

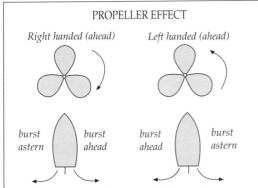

PROPELLER EFFECT

Right handed (ahead)   *Left handed (ahead)*

burst astern   burst ahead   burst ahead   burst astern

The effect is maximised when the ship is hardly moving. A 3-bladed propeller has more influence than a 2-bladed one. The rudder has little effect as the ship is not making way.

found it to be the *only* way in a strong crosswind. A snag arises when you come to rig the passerelle, but it is not insuperable and you can always climb over the pulpit!

A second snag of berthing bow-to is the task of handling your anchor over the stern when your windlass, anchor and chain are all up forward. No doubt you will find a way round the problem but it is a self-inflicted complication.

Stern-to makes getting away much easier and the passerelle is easily rigged but, unless you have a central cockpit, you are in the public eye. We are rarely bothered by the passing throng and have developed several ways of

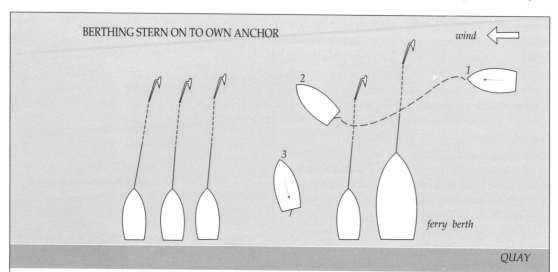

BERTHING STERN ON TO OWN ANCHOR   *wind*   *ferry berth*   QUAY

1. Having assessed the position, the Skipper decides on a down-wind approach: the wind and his propeller effect will help him to swing and offset the problem posed by the larger yacht.
2. Yacht stops with bow over position for anchor. Let go. Engine astern, helm to starboard in an attempt to correct over-swing.
3. Coming in nicely — but should he have reversed his helm? No!

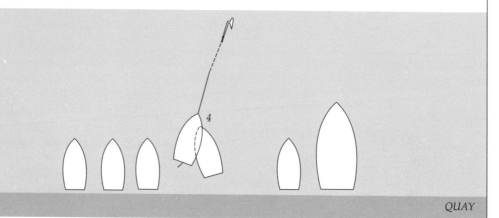

QUAY

4. Reversed helm and a gust of wind causes over-swing. Checks cable, gives a sharp burst ahead which thrusts stern to starboard without driving yacht ahead. Resumes slow astern and in...

getting rid of people who are too intrusive!

Many marinas now use "lazy lines" — mooring chains led to the quay or pontoon by lines which you pick up. You go bow or stern in to the allocated berth, get a line ashore, pick up a lazy line with your boathook (often it is handed to you by an attendant) and take it hand-over-hand to the stern (or bow as appropriate). Wear industrial gloves unless you have very tough hands as the line can be encrusted with barnacles. Haul it in until it is sufficiently tight to hold you off the quay and make fast. (This is an operation when the warping drum on your electric windlass can be a boon). The line which leads the mooring chain to the quay remains attached there so that, when the time comes to sail, you simply drop the chain, let the line sink before you use your engine and away you go. With all end-on berthing, make sure you have ample fenders ranged on both sides. In a crosswind you may well land gently against the boat downwind of you: this is not unusual and no one objects provided you are well fendered and take up your own weight on your lines as soon as possible.

Berthing "end-on" to your own anchor is not quite so simple. First of all, don't rush it. Weigh up where you want to lie. Has that lovely empty space a 'no berthing' sign on it? Or, just as likely, is there a sewage outfall there? Will it perhaps obstruct a ferry berth? Look to see how any other yachts are lying — are their cables leading fairly straight out from them or hauling off to one side or the other? The

latter indicates the prevailing wind or current and you will need to take it into account when placing your anchor. Are there any yachts lying to rope rather than chain — if so you will have to be very careful with your engine movements to avoid catching their rodes with your propeller. (If you are lying to rope and see another yacht heading to berth alongside you, please slack away your rode until he is in. It will be appreciated and, what is more, may save your line from being cut.)

How is the bottom described in the pilot — good or bad holding? Will your patent anchor be reliable or should you resort to your Fisherman? Is there plenty of room to lay out a generous scope of chain? It is advisable to lay out more than you would if swinging freely as you will inevitably have a sideways load on the anchor. From where is the wind blowing, and if you are berthing stern-to at what angle should your ship be in relation to the quay when you let go? You have to allow both for propeller effect as you go astern and for the wind turning you and taking you bodily to leeward.

All of this may sound bad enough to put you off trying the manoeuvre. Truly it's not that bad: you do need to know your ship and how she behaves going slow astern and you must keep your cool and be prepared to abort your approach to do it again if things go wrong. Once the anchor is down and beginning to hold, you will find it assists steering. You'll soon be berthing like this with no hassle but always take it seriously, because the time you don't is the time things will really go wrong.

Remember the comments in Chapter 6 about electric windlasses which can be controlled from the steering position and which will pay out as well as haul in.

BELOW *When mooring up to a bollard pass the bight of your rope up through the bowline of the other boat. This will enable the other to leave without disturbing your line.*

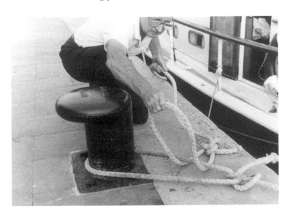

It may seem obvious to say you should have your lines ready before you berth, but you would be surprised how many people start to unravel tangled ropes when their stern is almost at the quay. If you can see the securing method used ashore, make your ropes ready appropriately: in other words, if you can see bollards are in use put good-sized bights on the ropes with bowlines, or if there is doubt just pass the rope end.

Getting the first line ashore and made fast with minimum delay is the prime object. If your line is heavy or has to be thrown some distance (e.g. over or past a dinghy in davits) you may choose to use a heaving line as a messenger. Most books on knots and hitches show you how to make a monkey's fist: put a round fishing weight inside it to help the line carry. Don't fuss about making up perfectly as you come alongside — you can adjust the lines in your own time once you are in.

Some people always make up with bowlines while others always bring their lines back on board. It's up to you, but bringing lines back on board does leave them subject to considerable chafe where they go round the bollards or through rings on the quay. Bowlines through rings also chafe but are the logical system with bollards. When making up to rings, we have found the round turn and two half-hitches to be very satisfactory, providing excellent security and no chafe.

If you are making up to a bollard using a bight, remember to feed your bight up through any others already using the same bollard before dropping it over. This allows other people who preceded you to recover their lines without disturbing yours.

When the time comes to sail, one line can be taken ashore and passed back on board, hauled really tight and made fast. Make sure it is free to run. Then the other shore lines can be taken in and stowed, the passerelle lifted and stowed and the single line slipped from one end when the order is given.

Lying alongside and unberthing

If you have to make up alongside a pier or piled quay, you will experience difficulty keeping your fenders in place. The secret is to have two planks (don't bother to varnish them!) each about 5 ft x 6 in (1.7 m x 15 cm) with a stout line attached to the top at each end. Two fenders are hung overside on either side of the pier leg or whatever and the

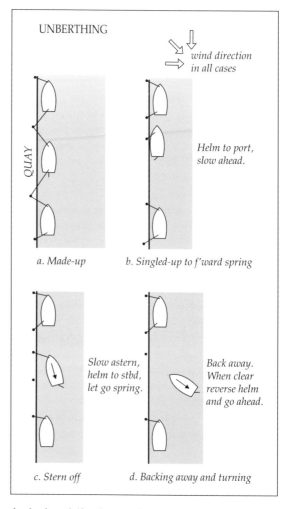

UNBERTHING

wind direction in all cases

Helm to port, slow ahead.

a. Made-up   *b. Singled-up to f'ward spring*

Slow astern, helm to stbd, let go spring.

Back away. When clear reverse helm and go ahead.

c. Stern off   *d. Backing away and turning*

fender board (for that is what we have just described) is then hung outside the fenders to bridge the gap between them and take the wear and tear without popping out.

To avoid chafing where lines pass over fairleads or rub against the edge of the quay, some short lengths of plastic tubing will do the trick.

If you are lying stern-to and a strong beam wind gets up, you may have to rig a long line from the bow (or at least from forward of amidships) to the quay at as broad an angle as possible to help hold the ship's head up to wind — assuming there is room to do so.

We briefly mentioned using a spring when berthing but this simple technique is even more useful when you are trying to get off a quay when there is not

much space to spare and/or when the wind is pinning you against it. The purpose of the exercise is to get your stern well off the quay so that you can back away before going ahead. Note that, unless there is someone ashore to cast off your spring, you will need to place it round the bollard (or through the ring) and return it back on board. In this case, make sure it will run freely when one inboard end is let go and that the line-handler moves fast when the order to let go is given.

Don't forget to place sufficient fenders well forward to protect your bow. If you've never sprung your ship off a quay, try it in quiet conditions. You will be surprised how far out the stern will move. It is far less work than using a boathook and is much more effective.

Ropes and lines

We have already referred to this subject in Chapter 5 but will amplify it a little here. Use lines of good weight — they are not much more expensive initially but will last considerably longer. Plaited lines for mooring are easier to handle than straight laid ones. Use the correct types of rope for each purpose — e.g. nylon for anchor rodes etc. Most rope manufacturers publish useful leaflets detailing which

ABOVE *This yacht badly needs fender boards to protect her topsides from the timber piles.*

BELOW *A laundry basket like this one provides practical stowage for mooring lines.*

ABOVE *Alternative rope stowage: a smart wooden locker on the foredeck for frequently used lines.*

materials are best for which purposes if you have doubts on the subject.

You must have enough to make up with the classic full set of head and stern ropes, breast ropes and springs. You won't always use the breast ropes but when you need them, you really do. Remember the long line (Chapter 5 and above). Have plenty of spare lines as all sorts of requirements will pop up: don't throw out anything until you are sure it has no residual use and this refers equally to old rope ends! If you are wondering where to stow all these ropes, the mooring lines which are used frequently can be stowed on deck in a plastic laundry basket if you have space, or hung on the guard rails.

Change the sheets and rope halyards end-to-end to spread the wear. Wash ropes and lines at least annually — they will be loaded with salt and sand. A good soaking and wash — or a spray with a high pressure cleaner (e.g. K'Archer, Hobby etc.) will be very beneficial. Indeed high-pressure water cleaners are extremely useful for all sorts of jobs on board.

Bosun's stores

You should have some commodious boxes or bags for the inevitable and essential bosun's bits and pieces. Make sure you have a good selection of shackles, several bulldog grips, a few carbine hooks, seizing wire (stainless steel and copper), gripfast and copper nails, a decent variety of s/s and brass or bronze screws, a good number of s/s hose clips of assorted sizes (it's truly amazing how many you can

use), whipping twines, self-amalgamating tapes, "Superglue", etc. In Appendix 6 we attempt to provide a comprehensive check list but the only thing we can be sure of is that it will not be complete!

It will probably be the bosun who goes up the mast. So what are our views on mast steps? We have never been shipmates with them nor felt we were missing anything. We use a soft-type bosun's chair (e.g. Simpson-Lawrence); we've used hard-seat types but found them to be very uncomfortable and awkward when aloft. The soft ones wrap themselves around you and give a secure feeling when you are swinging around the rigging. They let you use both hands, the chair has pockets for holding the bits and pieces needed and loops for tools. You will still experience that extraordinary feeling ("Oooh, that's nice") when your butt returns to life but all-in-all we continue to prefer a wrap-around chair to mast steps. The thought of going up the mast in a seaway is horrific in any circumstances; climbing up mast steps must be extremely difficult and hanging on when you get to the working spot totally impossible!

After a spell in continuous hot weather, the first heavy rain may well find some deck leaks caused by shrinkage — particularly if have you have wood beading along deck-to-coaming joints. You are most unlikely to cure the original leak by removing the beading and re-bedding it; in fact you are far more likely to make five new leaks! But a system passed on to us many, many years ago by a real shipwright on the East Coast of England works like a dream.

This is the "gunge gun": essentially a lever-action grease gun modified with the aid of a large brass or bronze countersunk-head screw. By large we mean at least 1/4 in (6 mm). The screw is drilled from its head through to its point giving a hole of about 1/8 in (3 mm). The screw head is then brazed carefully to the end of the grease gun (having removed the normal fitting which locks on to the grease nipples). This adaptation work can be given to a workshop — it is simple if you have the right tools but not many of us have a pillar-stand drill and a brazing torch.

To use the gunge gun, fill it with a mixture of a conventional flexible sealing compound such as "Seelastik", slightly thinned with heavy grease. You will have to experiment with the mix ratio — you need just enough to allow the sealant to pass through the gun and drilled screw under pressure. Drill two holes diagonally through the

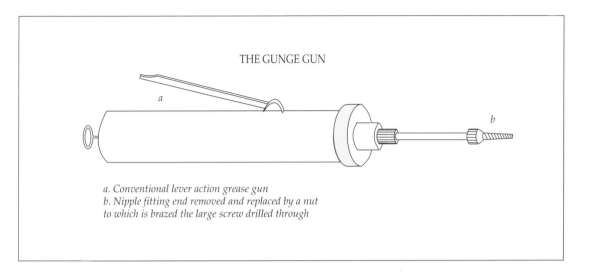

THE GUNGE GUN

a

b

a. Conventional lever action grease gun
b. Nipple fitting end removed and replaced by a nut
to which is brazed the large screw drilled through

ABOVE *The gunge gun — a grease gun modified to inject sealer deep into the boat's seams and crevices.*

beading on either side of the suspected leak and about 15 in (40 cm) apart. Take care not to drill deeper than the beading. The holes should be sufficiently large to accept the gunge gun screw — that is, to let it screw in firmly without cracking the beading.

Insert the gun into one of the holes and pump slowly, and the sealant will be injected under pressure. It will spread along the joint and very probably traces of it will squiggle out along the length of the beading until it emerges boldly from the second hole you drilled. You then know that you have filled the area where the leak would appear to be. However, knowing how far water will flow with capillary action, you may decide to extend the operation a little further in each direction.

Regrettably, if your yacht is all GRP and has deck/coaming leaks this will not work. Do not despair! We have found that "Captain Tolley's Creeping Crack Cure" is excellent for small leaks in any material as it too works on capillary action, traces the path taken by the water and penetrates even hairline fissures which it seals and bonds. It is probably available (maybe under another name) in many countries. However we are not sure that the US "Gluvit Epoxy Sealer" is quite the same thing.

A couple of snatch blocks are very useful to have; they can be used to adjust rope leads for all sorts of purposes — such as using the electric windlass to haul someone up the mast. A little ingenuity with snatch blocks can help you with all sorts of other problems too.

Have the longest (floating) boathook you can conveniently stow.

Regarding anti-foulings, you will find that locally made anti-foulings are usually cheaper and frequently more effective than the better-known yacht brands. Other yachties who know the local waters are bound to express their (varied!) opinions.

If you have much varnish work, you will need to watch it as sun and salt will attack it mercilessly. You may have to give it a rub-down and a couple of coats in mid-season. We have found that "International" Swedish Wood Oil finished off with a couple of coats of their U.V. varnish seems to work well. Undoubtedly, washing-off with fresh water is also a great help towards the prevention of varnish breakdown: water from rinsing out clothes can usefully be recycled in this way.

For cleaning off topsides, cabin coamings etc., and to remove dirt and oil stains, a mild solution of oxalic acid in water with a small amount of detergent is very good. Apply it with "Scotchbrite" or similar pads, leave it a few minutes then rinse off thoroughly. (You can buy ready-mixed concentrates such as "Sudbury Boat Zoap" marketed by Rule Industries Inc.) A similar solution, or a simple dilution of oxalic acid in water, is also very effective in removing rust stains and for bleaching wooden decks — but do not use it to clean fabrics.

An automobile exhaust (muffler) repair bandage — the type one wets and wraps round the fractured pipe then sets with heat — is useful for patching up damaged steel, copper, and rigid (but not flexible) plastic pipes. Alternatively, wrapping aluminium self-adhesive tape round the defect and then (if it is felt necessary) reinforcing it with resin-impregnated glass mat works well. On one of our previous yachts, the exhaust pipe disintegrated just downwind of the silencer: a GRP repair as above not only got us home but it lasted until the end of the season. If the fractured pipe is not under high pressure or heat, aluminium or plastic tape covered with two or three thicknesses of self-amalgamating tape will hold well.

It's amazing what repairs one can do using the modern "superglues" — either temporarily repairing the broken metal or plastic component or fabricating a new part. We once made a new brush holder for an electric bilge pump which worked for several weeks as necessary until we could buy a new pump. "Superglue" will also bond rubber, as when making new rubber seals from sheet or strip rubber. There are several variants of this product — one for rubber, pottery, aluminium, steel and most plastics; one for glass; and a gap-filling variety. However, as noted earlier, do not use it where direct heat is likely to be used (such as a soldering iron): under such conditions it can give off cyanide gas.

The real secret of a successful bosun is his "wot-not" box containing all those bits and pieces that must come in handy sometime, lesser mortals call it rubbish! Ours goes back thirty-plus years — and we regularly find just what we want among its contents!

As to "chandlery items", their availability varies enormously. It seems to us that many yacht chandlers in the popular cruising grounds tend to stock lots of exotic items but few pieces of basic hardware. Notable exceptions are in Cyprus, Gibraltar and at a few of the major French and Spanish marinas. It's always worthwhile seeking out what you want in hardware stores — especially in fishing ports as they stock many of the basics for the fishermen. What's more, the hardware is not all dressed up in fancy packaging and sold at inflated prices!

Security

Old Joshua Slocum's security system (the deck sprinkled with copper tacks every night) certainly coped well with the Indians of Tierra del Fuego but wouldn't achieve much nowadays! There are various intruder alarms on the market with wide price differentials. As you will normally have every door, hatch and port open when at anchor or in port, the concealed pressure mat or magnetic contact is probably largely ineffectual. An infra-red sensing system would seem to be the most attractive option and you can rig one up using one, two or more sensors to cover not only the accommodation but also the deck. The system should be one which turns itself 'off' and resets after a reasonable period of screeching. It should set off a very loud siren

(loud enough to be painful for those in close proximity) and perhaps switch on the deck (spreader) lights and possibly a flashing strobe light too. Thomas Walker's "Watchman" system, while expensive, meets these specifications and also is capable of accommodating pressure pads. What's more, the same control box can sound a warning of propane/butane gas presence, high engine temperature, high bilge water level and low battery power, so it is a fairly comprehensive system. Unfortunately, of course, the intruder alarm cannot differentiate between a rogue and the ship's cat which is a problem we have yet to surmount!

Some places house dens of thieves — the Mediterranean coasts of France and Italy, for example — but the less developed spots do not pose the same problems. The yachtie network will update you on local conditions. We have to say that, France excepted, we have hardly lost anything and we've only taken modestly sensible precautions. In some places, it is a good idea to engage a "local" as watchman: it rarely costs much (and he does precious little watching) but his employment is soon known along the waterfront and his integrity is respected. In the poorer countries, yachties are considered to be wealthy so don't behave provocatively by leaving cameras and what-have-you lying around, although the local people in such countries are usually naturally honest.

We always try to have some little "give-aways" on board for the children who will want to practise their English on you. Boiled sweets, stickers of your national flag, stick pins, picture postcards of your country and so on usually go down well. Friendliness towards the locals should be your natural attitude: it makes life so much more pleasant and a can of beer shared with a fisherman is invariably enjoyable as well as helping to maintain a good atmosphere between the communities. This, in turn, helps with the security aspects.

Save your copper tacks for their proper use!

POSTSCRIPT

So there you have it: a segment of our experiences and thoughts on the full-time cruising life.

We repeat the warning in our Preface — please don't be put off by our lists: they are not exclusive and there are a number of yachties who are thoroughly enjoying themselves with few or none of the "Nice to Haves" and perhaps (at their own risk) not all of the 'essentials'.

Many of us began life that way and have been able to add items little-by-little. At many of the more popular 'wintering' places, the yachties hold sales of surplus gear among themselves and it is often possible to pick up bargains there as well as to dispose of your own "unwanteds". At one such sale, one boat had no less than three — yes three! — sextants to sell. We've seen gas detectors, portable generators, compasses and all sorts on offer.

If you go ahead GOOD LUCK AND FAIR WINDS and we sincerely hope our efforts will prove to be of value to you.

APPENDICES

Appendix 1   Basic Galley Equipment

Hot and cold water, salt water

Drinking water tap if possible, with special filter; if electric pump installed, have a standby foot pump

Stove (+ grill), 4-burner if possible

Oven, if room

1 Fire blanket

Refrigerator and freezer (really almost obligatory if you are going to sail for hot climates — it's amazing where you can squeeze them in, particularly eutectic freezers)

Sink, oblong if possible

1 Good basic cookbook

1 Washing up bowl (plastic, to fit your galley sink)

1 Vacuum flask, pump action if possible*

1 Pressure cooker

1 Deep saucepan and lid

1 Large, family size, deep frying pan and lid

1 Non-stick milk pan

(N.B. A set of 3 x three cornered pans which fit on one stove ring are useful instead of separate pans)

1 Whistling kettle, either with no lid (fill from spout) or with a locking lid (to save spills)

1 Oven thermometer if no thermostat on the oven

1 Bread baking tin

1 Round cake tin

1 Swiss roll tin (useful for grilling items as well)

1 Bun tin (if required)

---

* Pump action flasks are invaluable for keeping water hot for quite some time. Since you pump the water out the lid does not have to be removed. Use them for mid-morning coffee or other hot drinks and for overnight passages when you can rustle up a quick 'Cup o' Soup' while on watch. However, we know that at present, in UK certainly, these are hard to come by. They are available in Spain. We set such store by them we would advise anyone contemplating setting off in any boat at any time to buy one whenever and wherever they are lucky enough to see one. If, in the end you change your mind, you can always use it at home!

1 Roasting tin (as large as the oven will take)

1 Plastic shaker (for mixing sauces etc.)

1 Fit-on-the-wall rubbish disposal bin (size to fit supermarket bags if possible as you always have lots of those)

1 Chopping board

1 Pair kitchen scissors

Serving plates (2)

Minimum of four of each of the following:

Cups/mugs

Large plates

Side plates

Soup/cereal/pudding plates

Egg cups

Glasses

Soup spoons

Pudding spoons

Tea spoons

Knives

Forks

1 Set salad servers

2 Serving spoons

1 Slotted spoon

1 Fish slice

1 Wooden spoon

1 Rolling pin (if you bake often, otherwise use a bottle filled with cold sea water and stoppered tightly)

3 Sharp knives (1 large, 1 medium, 1 small)

1 Tin opener

1 Vegetable peeler

1 Corkscrew/bottle opener

1 Plastic strainer (this is not good for straining hot fat but it does not rust as metal ones do)

2 or 3 Skewers

1 Set measuring spoons and cups

1 Measuring jug (if possible with Imperial and Metric quantities)

1 Pastry-mixing/salad bowl

Plastic film

Foil

Small and large plastic bags

Kitchen bin bags (for emergencies — mostly you will have
supermarket bags in plenty)

Dustbin bags (to pack away unwanted clothes)

Snap-shut plastic bags (they keep things dry beautifully)

Good quality plastic containers, assorted as required (eg.
Stewart or Tupperware)

Oven roasting bags (keep oven clean)

Knife sharpener (try to 'borrow' the Skipper's
permanently!)

1 Milk jug

1 Sugar shaker (not elegant but saves spills)

1 Small set of scales (if you use them)

1 Paper towel holder (if space allows)

Paper towels

Wash cloths or brush

N.B. When considering your choice of crockery Melamine
wear is pretty and hard wearing, as is stainless steel.
Stainless steel is particularly good for serving plates, salad
bowls etc. Stainless steel "glasses" are also available, as are
strong and attractive plastic ones.

"Nice to Have" (depending on cost and space)

Spin dryer (definitely our first luxury choice if space allows)

Small washing machine (eg. ITT Miniwash) (but remember
water consumption)

Mini food processor or blender

Coffee maker (the metal Italian filter type is neat, makes
good coffee and doesn't break easily)

Sandwich toaster (either manual to use on top of the stove or
electric)

Mincer

Vacuum sweeper (if you have carpets)

Microwave oven

Appendix 2   Basic Food Supplies

(For more information see *The Beaufort Scale Cookbook*, also published by Fernhurst.)

Dry or storable goods

Flour
Salt
Pepper
Mustard
Sugar
Tea
Coffee (instant and ground)
Tomato sauce
Other sauces (barbecue, H.P. soya etc)
Mayonnaise, salad dressing
Pickles/chutney
Curry powder
Dry/UHT milk
Drinking chocolate/cocoa
Jams/marmalade/honey
Sweet and savory biscuits/crispbreads
Pastas/sago/semolina/ground rice
Rice (pudding and long grain/basmati)
Cornflour
Stock cubes
Cereals
English custard powder
Bread crumbs
Dry herbs/spices (small quantities — in general they do not keep well, specially spices)
Cooking oil/tinned fat and margarine/olive oil
Lemon juice
Marmite/Bovril/Vegemite
Syrup/treacle
Porridge oats
Dry vegetables (peas, beans etc)
Dry potato
Pulses (lentils, beans, chick peas, barley etc.)
Sultanas, raisins, currants
Nuts
Gravy powder
Vinegar

Essences
Dried quick-action yeast
Jellies or other packet puddings
Packet soups
Fruit juices
Nibbles of your choice (olives, crisps, mini biscuits etc.)
Large pre-made rich fruit cake

Tinned supplies

Soups
Fish, various
Shellfish, various
Cooked meats, various
Cooked cold meats, various
Ham, luncheon meat
Pates
Made-up sauces, or other dishes
Pie fillings, sweet and savory
Puddings, various
Milk, condensed/evaporated/dry
Cream
Made-up English custard
Fruit, various
Sauces (apple etc.)

Drinks

Squashes/other soft drinks
Mixers, Colas, Beers, Wines, Cider
Hard liquor as required
Bottled water

Fresh foods

Eggs, Butter, Cheeses, Milk, Yoghurts
Margarine/lard/fat
Bread/rolls
Salad vegetables
Potatoes, Onions, Fresh vegetables, Fresh fruit
Fish
Sausages, Meat, Bacon
Cold meats/meat pies
Root ginger

Appendix 3   Notice to joining crew

Welcome on board! Please read the following notes.

1. Fire extinguishers are located in each compartment:

Forecabin : under seat forward

Saloon : by door to engine room

Deck saloon : by chart table

After cabin : by mizzen post

Engine room and generator room (Lazarette) have automatic fire extinguishers plus one manual extinguisher just to left inside engine room door.

2. Lifejackets and safety harness are stowed in the box beneath the wheel, as are flares.

3. Liferaft is on starboard-side of after coachroof. It contains an emergency pack but bring your own Scotch.

4. An emergency position indicating radio beacon (EPIRB) is to port-hand of the wheel. Instructions for use are on it.

5. Water: the ship carries about 200 gallons (900 lts.) fresh water which is ample for prudent consumption. However — please do not leave taps running unnecessarily — e.g. while cleaning your teeth. When showering, wet yourselves then turn the shower off while you soap and then turn on shower again to sluice off. Please don't wash your hair every day. Drinking water is drawn from the appropriately marked tap in the galley. This is filtered against bacteria.

6. Clothing: Wear as much or as little as you will. Do not bother to dress for evening cocktails.

7. Laundry: The Chief Steward will notify you of laundry arrangements. There is a washing machine and spin-dryer on board (to be operated only by the Chief Steward).

8. There is a spare blanket under each bunk in the forecabin should you feel chilly at night.

9. Bar: Feel free to help yourself from the fully stocked bar. If taking cans or bottles from the deck refrigerator (located abaft of the wheelhouse on port side) please replenish from the ship's stocks (forward port locker in wheelhouse).

10. Deck Loungers: two foam rubber mattresses and two lilos are available for lying on deck. Please do not use the green cloth-covered ones when wet after swimming but do use them for sun-bathing (after spreading a towel over them if you are using sun oil/cream). The grey plastic lilo may be used in the water but not, please, the blue material one.

11. Main W.C.: this is operated by closing the lid and pushing the large white button behind it to the left. The cycle takes about three minutes before the vacuum is released and the lid can be opened. Please do not put heavy paper, kitchen towels, any type of sanitary towel or other such material in the W.C. as these will block it. Please ask the Chief Steward about disposal of any awkward items. Should you find the loo blocked (i.e. with paper still in the bowl or no water evident) please inform the Chief Steward at once and she will (reluctantly!) clear it.

12. Shower: to empty, please switch on the brown switch on side of the airing cupboard. As the water will remain in the shower until pumped out, there is no need to use the plug. Please ensure the round plastic filter is over the outlet to catch hair which would otherwise eventually jam the pump. After using the bath, please use a piece of toilet paper to wipe round the plastic filter to remove any hair and place it in the waste bin on the engine room door in the galley area. Do not put it in the loo.

13. If any guest feels in the least sea-sick, please ask the Chief Steward for a Stugeron tablet at once.

14. Navigational Equipment: The Navigating Officer has requested that the following notice, which applies to all electronic equipment, be drawn to the attention of all unqualified personnel:

ACHTUNG! ALLES TURISTEN UND NON-TECHNISCHTEN LOOKENPEEPERS

Das machine kontrol is nicht fur gerfingerpoken und mitten-grabben uderwise is easy schnappen de springwerk, blowenfuse und poppencorken mit spitsensparken. Das machine ist diggen by expertzen only, ist nicht fur gerwerken by das dumkopfen. Der rubbernecken seemen keepen das cottonpicken hands in das pockets so relaxen und watchen das blinken lights.

15. Telephone: Radio-telephone facilities to UK/Continent are available subject to atmospheric conditions. Please discuss your requirements with the Master, Chief Engineer or Radio Officer. Costs are for caller's account; reverse charges may be available.

16. Personal accident, loss and theft liability: We regret that neither the ship nor her owners are liable for the costs and/or consequences of personal accident, theft or loss. Crew and visitors are recommended to arrange their own insurance and to take all reasonable precautions.

We hope you thoroughly enjoy your crewing with us. Kindly complete the slip herewith and hand it to the Master, Chief Officer or Chief Steward as soon as convenient so that your details may be added to the Crew List.

Appendix 4 Spare Parts and Consumables Checklist

Engine

1 set injectors (for each engine)

1 fuel lift pump overhaul kit

1 water-pump impeller (for each pump and spare F.W. circulating pump if of integral type)

Lengths, various diameters, rubber hoses to fit

1 set cylinder head gaskets

Gasket material (for making misc. gaskets)

Fibre washers, miscellaneous sizes

Sealing rubber for heat exchanger(s)

Fuel filter elements (suggest 3 of each type min.)

Oil filter elements (suggest 3 of each type min.)

Lubricating oil for topping-up & 1 oil change

Tachometer drive cable (if relevant)

Alternator and power offtake drive belts

Length suitable fuel piping

Thermostat

Outboard motor sparking plugs

Outboard motor sheer-pins/drive springs (if relevant)

Instruments

Instrument panel(s) pilot light bulbs

Fascia light bulbs (if appropriate)

Fuses (including 'specials' — see instruments' manuals)

Special papers (e.g. for Navtex, barograph, etc.)

Towing log — line, sinker and impeller

Thru'hull log impeller

Thru'hull log drive cable (if relevant)

Electrical

Fuse wire

Assorted fuses

Strips of cable joiners (large, medium, small)

Assorted lengths of cable — various gauges

Assorted D.C. & A.C. light bulbs to fit

Navigation light bulbs (10 & 20 watt)

2-3 assorted switches (D.C. & A.C.)

2-3 assorted sockets (D.C. & A.C.)

Fresh-water pump overhaul kit — diaphragm; pulsation dampeners; drive belt; pressure switch

5 litres (10 pints) battery water

Bilge pump

Insulating tape

Cable clips

Assorted shore cable plugs

Batteries for misc. portable equipment (e.g. torches etc.)

Other

W.C. overhaul kit (incl. 1 set seat seals if appropriate)

Hand pump overhaul kits

Fresh-water filter elements

Packing for stern gland(s) etc.

Washers — taps, hot & cold water

Appendix 5 Tool List

Engine

1 set open & ring spanners (imperial & metric)

1 set sockets with ratchet drive, universal drive and extension rod (imperial & metric)

1 set allen keys (imperial & metric)

1 "King Dick" type adjustable wrench — large

1 "King Dick" type adjustable wrench — medium

1 "King Dick" type adjustable wrench — small

1 pipe wrench

1 "Stillson" — large

1 "Stillson" — small

1 Philips screwdriver — medium

1 Philips screwdriver — small

Screwdrivers, various sizes incl. 1 large with long shaft

1 filter strap

1 rubber or hide mallet

1 wire brush

1 oil can

1 grease gun

Deck

1 portable vice

1 double-sided (coarse/fine) carborundum sharpening stone

1 set wood chisels (6mm/ $\frac{1}{4}$", 12mm/ $\frac{1}{2}$", 25mm/ 1", 40mm/ 1 $\frac{1}{2}$")

1 set cold chisels (small to medium)

1 ball-pein hammer (medium — say 500g/ 1lb)

1 light tacking hammer

1 club hammer (2kg/ 4lbs min.)

1 6mm/ $\frac{1}{4}$" hand drill (wheel-brace)

1 electric drill of appropriate voltage — min. 10mm/ $\frac{3}{8}$" chuck

Assorted high-speed twist drills

1 set hole saws (up to 50mm/ 2" at least)

Countersink bit(s)

1 general-purpose saw (e.g. "Eclipse", available with spare blades)

1 hacksaw (with spare blades)

1 carpenter's brace

Assorted wood bits

1 folding or flexible rule (metric and imperial)

1 padsaw or "keyhole" saw with spare blades

1 bradawl

1 centre-punch

1 small nail punch

1 flat file

1 half-round file

1 rat-tailed file

1 wood rasp (or "Surform" with both flat & quarter-round blades)

1 general-purpose steel plane (or "Surform")

1 round rasp (or "Surform")

1 pair medium pliers

1 pair fine-nosed pliers

1 pair "tinman's" snips or shears (medium-size)

1 set taps & dies (say to 10mm/ $\frac{3}{8}$")

1 set "jeweller's" screwdrivers

1 "Stanley" knife (with spare blades)

1 pair wire cutters — large (to deal easily with thickest rigging wire on board)

1 axe — medium weight

Paint scrapers and "Skarsten" scrapers

1 electrician's terminal crimping set

1 pair electrician's "side-cutters"

1 electrician's screwdriver

1 soldering iron (with multi-core solder — also plumber's solder & flux

1 gas blowlamp and brazing kit (with paint-removing nozzle) & spare gas cylinders (e.g. "Camping Gaz")

1 multimeter (or at least a simple continuity tester)

NOTE: Believe it or not, the above is a reasonable tool kit. Many boats carry considerably more and you will probably find yourself borrowing and/or buying other items!

Appendix 6   Bosun's and Carpenter's Locker

Acetone, large tin/bottle

Blocks, assorted as appropriate

Snatch blocks — 2

Bolts, nuts & washers, s/s., relevant assortment

Bosun's chair

Buckets, with lanyards — 2

Bulldog clips (several to fit standing rigging sizes)

Small ball caulking cotton

Codline (for lacings, lashings etc.)

Deck caulking mastic (synthetic rubber)

Deck scrubber

Elastic cord, assorted sizes — 1 m (3 ft) of each

Eyelets, brass, with punch kit

Funnels, plastic (1 large, 1 small)

GRP gelcoat repair paste (if appropriate)

GRP filler — smooth and chopped mat reinforced

Glue, instant "Superglue" type

Glue, wood

Grease, general purpose for deck use

Hose, plastic — short lengths various diameters

Hose clips, s/s, a good number and variety of sizes

Hosepipe fittings, assorted

"Jerrycans", plastic, 2 x 22 ltr (5 gall) for fuel

Kerosene — 2.5 ltr (5 pints)

Keys: spares for deck filler caps

Linseed oil (boiled & raw), large bottle/tin of each

Methylated spirit — large tin/bottle

Oil, freeing/penetrating

Oxalic Acid (for cleaning paintwork, bare wood, teak etc.); 2 ltr (3-4 pints)

Oil, light lubricating — 1 large-sized tin

PTFE (plumber's) tape

Petroleum jelly — anhydrous (e.g. "Vaseline") — large jar/tin

Plugs, several wooden, various sizes

Rags, good supply

Resin, and glass mat (coarse & fine)

Rigging screws (suggest 2 of general-purpose size)

Rod, threaded s/s., approx. 50 cm (18 in) of each of 6 mm ($^1/_4$ in) and 10 mm ($^3/_8$ in) with 10 nuts and washers to fit each

Rope & line ends worth keeping

Rope — spare lengths to renew sheets/halyards as assessed

Sailmaker's needles, assorted

Sailmaker's palm

Sailmaker's spike

"Scotchbrite" (or similar) cleaning pads, 1 pack

Screws, self-tapping s/s, c'sunk and cheese heads

Screws, wood: good assortment bronze/brass & s/s; countersunk and round heads

Screw eyes & hooks, various sizes; s/s or brass

Scrubbing brush

"Seelastik" or similar flexible sealant

Shackles, stainless steel, assorted "D" & bow

Sheeting, plastic — at least 1 piece 3 x 2 m (10 ft x 6 in) or equivalent for covering items on deck, etc. The green plastic garden sheets already eyeletted are excellent

Seizing wire — 1 spool stainless steel; 1 spool copper

Sponge, large

Tapes, plastic

Tapes, self-amalgamating

Teak Cleaner (powder or liquid, or see oxalic acid above)

Thimbles, assorted stainless steel

Threads and whipping twines (waxed and plain)

Torch, powerful waterproof

Water carriers, folding plastic, 2 x 22 ltr (5 gall) for carrying drinking water

Water repellant spray (e.g. WD40)

Wedges, wooden, various sizes

Wet & dry sandpaper — coarse, medium and fine

White spirit (thinners No.1) — 2.5 ltrs (5 pints)

Winch handles, one spare of each size

Wire, flexible s/s, a length for rigging repair

Appendix 7 Basic Medical Supplies

Equipment
First aid book
Space blanket (for hypothermia, shock and just to keep warm when necessary)
Safety pins, assorted
3 bandage clips
1 pair scissors
1 pair tweezers
1 thermometer
3 hypodermic syringes and needles (disposable)

Bandages etc.
Several rolls of bandage in assorted sizes
Several rolls of tube gauze in assorted sizes
Finger stalls
1 eye shield
1 sling
Several butterfly adhesive strips (to close wounds)
1 crepe bandage
6 sterile dressings
1 tube Opsite liquid skin
Elastoplast — assorted sizes
Elastoplast — strip to cut to size as required
2 rolls adhesive tape (thick and thin)
Gauze
Cotton wool
Lint
Elastic bandages for elbows, wrists, knees or ankles if you think you may require them

Antiseptics and healing remedies
Antiseptic wipes
Antiseptic powder
Antiseptic liquid (TCP or Dettol etc.)
Arnica homeopathic tablets (for bruises and wounds)
Arnica homeopathic ointment for bruises (NOT wounds)
Nelson's homeopathic ointment for cuts and sores
Other antiseptic creams

Ears
Ear drops
Cotton buds

Eyes
Optrex
Eye bath
Eye drops
Eye ointment
Contact lens solutions if used

Nose and throat
Piriton (or other) tablets for hayfever (homeopathic "mixed pollen" tablets are also good)
Cold remedy
Cough mixture

Mouth and teeth
Oil of cloves (for toothache)
D.I.Y. tooth repair kit
Bonjela
Dental floss or similar

Painkillers
Aspirin/paracetamol etc.
Nurofen for more severe pain
DF 118 for very severe pain (ask your G.P.)
Migraleve (or similar — for migraine)

Seasickness
Stugeron
Seabands

Burns
Burn dressings
Burn ointment
Several tubes Nelson's homeopathic burn ointment. We recommend this as a fast relief from pain.

Sunburn

Cream/oil/lotion in various strengths

Aftersun cream/lotion

Sunglasses!

Antibiotics and stomach complaint remedies

Tetracycline (see your G.P.)

Shock remedy (see your G.P.)

Worm tablets (specially Pripsen, for tape worm)

Arret or similar for diarrhoea

Kaolin morph. mixture

Natural laxative

Bicarbonate of soda

Asilone or Aludrex tablets (or similar) for indigestion

Alka Seltzer or Andrews Liver Salts

Other medical stores

Re-hydration tablets or crystals

Calcium tablets

Cool wipes

Sting relief such as Wasp Eze

Insect repellant

Vaseline Tineafax (for foot fungus)

DON'T FORGET any medication you require yourselves.

Personal hygiene

Toothbrushes

Nail brushes

Face flannels

Soap

Toothpaste

Shampoo

Hair conditioner

Hair setting lotion

Hair brushes and combs

Talc

Deodorants

Shaving gear and soap

Sanitary towels

Paper tissues

Appendix 8 Basic Household Items

Reusable paper towels (if you can find them)

Scrubbing brush

Rubber gloves

J-Cloths

Floor cloth

Chamois leather

Dust pan

Soft brush

Stiff brush

Several assorted buckets (plastic and preferably with plastic handles and including one very large one for cleaning ropes, soaking laundry etc.)

Clothes line (of good length)

Clothes pegs (firm-holding type)

Soap

Washing up liquid

Washing powder

Stain remover (eg. Beckman, Vanish, Biotex)

Soap pads

Lavatory brush

Lavatory cleaner

Air freshener

Toilet rolls

Polishes as required

Mosquito coils/spray/electric pads

Rodent poison

Cockroach hives

Insect killing spray

Matches

Candles

Shower cleaner

Ammonia

Bleach

Potassium permanganate or Milton

Dusters

Cold bag to carry home food

Shopping bag/trolley (see text, Chapter 7)

Window cleaner

"Stay-Fresh" bags, or similar

Paper napkins

Household linen (sheets, pillowslips, table mats, towels, hand towels, tea towels, face flannels, blankets or sleeping bags and don't forget pillows — mattresses will probably already be in situ)

Oven mitt

Deck broom

Non-slip mats or material

Household cleaners as required

Stationery as required

Pet food, litter etc. if required

A good old-fashioned fly swat if you can find one!

ACKNOWLEDGEMENTS

Our very grateful thanks are extended to all our cruising friends of many nationalities who, knowingly or unknowingly, have helped us to continue the learning process which never ends in this pastime of ours. Some of the ideas which we are passing on have originated with them, as has the knowledge in fields of which we were previously ignorant. All the suggestions and opinions we have expressed in this volume are our sole responsibility and if they don't work for you or if you disagree with them, shoot at us!

In particular we would like to express our appreciation to Erik Fokke, lately of the good ship *Ferrosimo*, for so kindly agreeing to our use of a very illuminating survey he carried out at Larnaca Marina, Cyprus, over the winter of 1990/91.

The assistance of the Royal Yachting Association is gratefully recognised for allowing us to quote their formula for calculating the lengths of chain or rope/chain recommended for anchoring to most efficient effect (Chapter 10). Their booklets, in this instance *Cruising Yacht Safety*, are well worth study.

It is appropriate here to make it totally clear that the references in the text to various manufacturers, suppliers and equipment are included simply to give reference points to readers. We do not intend to imply in any way that those mentioned are superior to others or, conversely, that those not mentioned are inferior in any way whatsoever. All such specific references are totally of our own free choice.

Finally our limitless thanks to our offspring, Shirley and Christopher, who have looked after our affairs in England with the very kind help of their friends and ours. Thank you also to those who helped with urgently-needed spares, including our visitors who, only too often, found their baggage allowance used up before they had begun to pack their own clothes! We loved having them on board with or without the bits of engine!

INDEX

ALSO PUBLISHED BY FERNHURST BOOKS

The Beaufort Scale Cookbook *June Raper*
Boat Engines *Dick Hewitt*
Celestial Navigation *Tom Cunliffe*
Children Afloat *Pippa Driscoll*
Coastal and Offshore Navigation *Tom Cunliffe*
Cruising Crew *Malcolm McKeag*
Cruising Skipper *John Mellor*
Electronics Afloat *Tim Bartlett*
First Aid Afloat *Dr Robert Haworth*
Heavy Weather Cruising *Tom Cunliffe*
Inshore Navigation *Tom Cunliffe*
Knots and Splices *Jeff Toghill*
Log Book for Cruising under Power *Tom Willis & Tim Bartlett*
Log Book for Cruising under Sail *John Mellor*
Marine SSB Operation *Michael Gale*
Marine VHF Operation *Michael Gale*
Mental and Physical Fitness for Sailing *Alan Beggs et al*
Motor Boating *Alex McMullen*
Navigation at Speed *Tim Bartlett*
Powerboating *Peter White*
Racing Crew *Malcolm McKeag*
Racing Skipper *Robin Aisher*
Radar *Tim Bartlett*
The Rules in Practice 1993-96 *Bryan Willis*
Rules of the Road *John Mellor*
Sails *John Heyes*
Simple Electronic Navigation *Mik Chinery*
Tides and Currents *David Arnold*
Weather at Sea *David Houghton*

Fernhurst Books are available from all good bookshops and chandleries. In case of difficulty, or if you would like a copy of our full catalogue, please send your name and address to:
Fernhurst Books, 33 Grand Parade, Brighton, East Sussex BN2 2QA, UK